LIVING
a
PARABLE

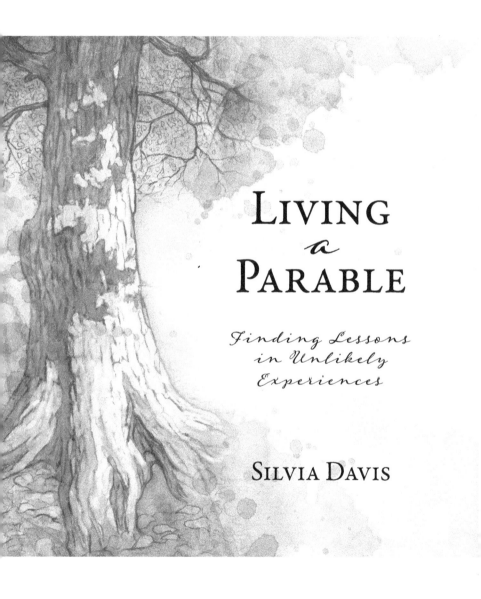

LIVING
a
PARABLE

*Finding Lessons
in Unlikely
Experiences*

SILVIA DAVIS

XULON PRESS

Xulon Press
2301 Lucien Way #415
Maitland, FL 32751
407.339.4217
www.xulonpress.com

Edited by Xulon Press

Unless otherwise indicated, Scripture taken from the NEW
AMERICAN STANDARD BIBLE ®, Copyright © 1960,1962,1
963,1968,1971,1972,1973,1975,1977,1995 by The Lockman
Foundation. Used by permission.

Paperback ISBN-13: 978-1-66281-898-1
Ebook ISBN-13: 978-1-66281-899-8

DEDICATION

I dedicate this book to my Lord. Through Him, all things are possible, and without Him, none of this would have been possible. Should this book entertain, help, or guide anyone, all praise and thanks are due Him.

TABLE OF CONTENTS

PREFACE

What is a parable? In a nutshell, parables are stories, or maybe even a simple verse, used to illustrate a lesson or a principle. Parables are used to make a complex lesson or message relatable and practical. Jesus masterfully used parables to build images and stories for His listeners, but here's the catch, He not only used them to reveal the truth, but He also used them to conceal the truth. Jesus used parables to hide His message from those He knew weren't open to receiving it. In Matthew 13:10-17, Jesus explained to His disciples why He used parables. Here's the first half of that passage:

> "And the disciples came and said to Him, 'Why do You speak to them in parables?' Jesus answered them, 'To you it has been granted to know the mysteries of the kingdom of heaven, but to them it has not been granted. For whoever has, to him more shall be given, and he will have an abundance; but whoever does not have, even what he has shall be taken away from him. Therefore, I speak to them in parables; because while seeing they do not see, and while hearing they do not hear, nor do they understand' "(Matt 13:10-13)

There is some controversy concerning exactly how many parables Jesus told. Still, one thing is sure, and that is Christ found parables to be an effective way to teach those who truly wanted to receive His message.

God is still teaching us today. Have you ever taken the time to look back at your life, searching for lessons you may have missed? Our lives are full of opportunities to learn and grow if we open ourselves up to them. The lessons may present themselves in melancholy, humorous, blatant, or subtle forms, but usually, somewhere within that experience lies an opportunity for growth.

My siblings and I joked for years concerning writing a book about our experiences as kids, but none of us could ever find the time to make it happen. Because of life's involuntary slow-down due to lockdowns and restrictions in 2020, this is that book.

1

The Cast

"We love, because He first loved us" (1 John 4:19).

My parents, Eldolgie and Annie, met as teens. They fell in love, got married, and started a family. In 1971, along came their first child—me. A year and a half later, my little sister, Leslie, was born. Seventeen months after Leslie, Lucretia was born. Three years after Lucretia, Eldolgina, or "Gina," was born, and 13 months after Gina, Wesley was born. I jokingly tell my siblings that I'm the blockbuster hit, and they are the sequels that could never live up to the original. Being a teen in the '80s was a fun time, and because of the dynamic of our family, friends often compared us to the *Cosby Show* kids.

Although Leslie is the second child, I feel she should have been the oldest. She is the mother hen of the group. Lucretia fits the definition of the middle child in every way there is. Gina was that tomboy rebel and, while I joke about my siblings being sequels, Wesley always says, "Mom and Dad kept going until they got it right." My dad, who everyone refers to as "Crawford," was a career military

1

man. Dad is also a God-fearing man, and his love for our Heavenly Father is immeasurable. My mother was a funny, stubborn, strong-willed woman who still maintains the adoration of all of her children. We, unfortunately, lost her in 2017.

We sometimes fought like cats and dogs in our family, but we were always there for each other when we needed each other. There were so many different personalities and so many people to love. The Crawford Family was and still is rock solid.

Attempting to recreate that same kind of family stability for myself proved to be more difficult than my parents made it seem, but I did find it in three very special people. I refer to them as My Three J's; my husband John, my son Jacob, and my daughter Jordan.

John takes care of me and gives me the confidence and support to do things that I would never even attempt without him. Jacob is the most sincere, honest, and pleasant man anyone could ever hope to meet. Jordan is my ambitious, determined mini-me, and she has me wrapped around her little finger, just as tightly today as she did the day she was born.

As I think of everyone I've just briefly told you about, I can't help but think of how God has used my interactions with them, both as a child and as an adult, to teach me some valuable lessons. God is always teaching. We aren't always aware of those lessons in the moment, but I bet if you took a minute to sit back and recollect on certain times in your life, you would be able to extract precious nuggets of knowledge. God's hand is in everything.

In this book, I share with you some of the lessons I extracted from my own life. Each chapter begins with an experience from the days I lived under my parent's roof, followed by a similar lesson learned from an adult perspective. These are lessons that apply to us all. After each lesson is a call to action, along with blank pages for you to jot down your thoughts, you will also find Bible scriptures to support the message and end each lesson with prayer.

I hope you are ready to study some, apply some, and relate some.

A Fight in a Tub

> "Cease from anger and forsake
> wrath; Do not fret; it leads only
> to evildoing" (Ps. 37:8).

Five children and one bathroom sink; this was the hardship we had to deal with in the Crawford house. I don't even know how in the world we survived. It wasn't uncommon for my sisters and me to share the mirror or sink while doing our hair and makeup. On this particular day, Gina and I were at odds. I can't remember why we were mad at each other, but we were. She was determined to make it difficult for me to do what I needed to do, which was use the sink. I turned the water on, and she turned it off. I turned the water on again, and she turned it off again. I took a deep breath, then turned the water back on. She immediately shut it off.

I decided not to escalate the situation. I was the oldest, and I would act like it; plus, I knew our parents disapproved of us arguing and fighting with each other. Once, when I was arguing with Leslie, our dad tried to convince us to stop by saying, "You're sisters! You're supposed to get along, not argue!"

I replied, "Daddy, you argue with mom sometimes, and you *picked* her." As Dad walked away, I'm sure I heard him say under his breath, "Carry on."

On this day, while battling over the sink with Gina, I told myself to let it go and walked over to the tub. I sat down on the edge of the tub, with my back to Gina, and turned on the water. I could see her shadow creeping up behind me. Gina's hand came from behind and reached around me to the knob for the tub. I remember this vividly because her hand was moving in slow motion. She turned the water off!

Unfortunately, I allowed my anger to get the best of me as I swung the first punch, without considering I was still sitting on the tub's edge. Gina swung back, and I fell on my back into the tub. I was throwing punches up, and she was throwing punches down. The six years of age that I had on her didn't matter much in that situation. She had determination and vantage point on her side.

That was years ago, and the passing of time is not why I cannot recall what led to the fight. The reason I can't remember is that it was unimportant and not worth arguing over in the first place.

When my son, Jacob, was five years old, we moved in with my parents for a year. During that time, Gina was also living there with her three-year-old daughter, Xamara. There are lots of great memories associated with that time. One of which was being able to spend a bit more time with my niece. I nicknamed Xamara, Anakin, as in Skywalker, from *Star Wars*. I felt Xamara was wise beyond her years, and if she didn't use her powers for good, she would fall over into the Dark Side.

Xamara was a master of compliments, as well as criticisms, even at such a young age. She was brutally vocal, as most children are who have not yet learned when to speak their mind or when to remain silent. There was a time, while in line at a grocery store with Gina, Xamara noticed the woman standing directly behind them and said, "You pretty."

The stranger said, "Thank you!"

Then, Xamara looked at the next woman in line and said, "And you pretty." Then she looked at the third woman in line. Xamara's expression completely changed from that of someone delivering good news to an expression that said, "Oh girl..." Her tiny jaw dropped as she let out a slight groan and then said to the woman, "And you *not* pretty."

Like I said, very open and honest about what she thought.

While my kids and I were living with my parents, I treated my niece like she was one of my kids in every way, including bedtime. My kids went to bed at 8 p.m. So when Xamara was left in my care, she also went to bed at 8 p.m. An 8 p.m. bedtime was earlier than usual for her. She became at such odds with me that she stopped calling me Auntie Silvia and began referring to me as Uncle's wife. Xamara was clearly frustrated with me, and since she couldn't unleash that frustration on me, I believe she lashed out at the only other person she could – Jacob. Xamara would do everything in her power to get under Jacob's skin, and since he was a bit more sensitive than I cared to admit, it worked for her.

Xamara was merciless. She would tell Jacob she was Grandma's favorite or his curly hair looked like worms on his head. Xamara became so comfortable with lashing out at him that it didn't even matter to her if I was in the room when she did it. She recognized that I had reached a point where it was more important to me that Jacob handle the situation without my interference.

I would constantly advise him to ignore her. I told him if he continued to let her see that she was getting to him, she would never stop. I wanted Jacob to learn this lesson early. I wanted him to learn what I learned the day I struggled to dodge blows from within a bathtub. I wanted him to understand that most situations aren't worth becoming upset over.

For weeks the teasing continued until one glorious day, the switch finally flipped! Xamara was teasing Jacob, as usual, but nothing she said upset or frustrated him. She told him he couldn't draw good, and he didn't cry. She told him he wasn't going to be tall when he grew up, and he said nothing; he didn't even glance in her direction. In desperation, Xamara reached way down deep into her bag of insults and yelled, "And your friends are ugly.... I seen 'em!"

That was a turning point, and Xamara was never again able to frustrate Jacob with her teasing.

Also, a few months after we moved out, Xamara did start calling me Auntie Silvia again!

THE LESSON

The year 2020 brought us an entire array of differences. We suddenly found ourselves divided concerning so many topics: mask or don't mask, actual virus or hoax, quarantine or don't quarantine, Trump, Biden, or Kanye West? In 2020 we saw so many people turn into three-year-old Xamaras. People spouted off whatever they felt like saying at the moment. They didn't care about who they might hurt, or worse, they made being hurtful the goal.

We tossed life-long relationships aside because of anger over a difference of opinions. That is not a Christian response. We are called to be above such nonsense.

Rather than remembering how much that person meant to us, we focused on their *wrong* view on a matter, and tempers flared. We attempted to justify our anger by saying it was a moral issue. Then we acted like no longer being part of their life was taking the moral high ground. In many cases, a difference in morals wasn't the issue; it was instead a difference in perceptions, experiences, and an inability to see things from the other side.

We aren't to be someone constantly seizing or creating opportunities to quarrel, nor are we to let our anger take control of us. There is a reason God's word tells us repeatedly to be slow to anger. Anger causes us to overreact and robs us of our ability to reason. In those moments before I took that first swing at my sister, I wasn't thinking. There were better ways I could have reacted in response to my anger. However, anger prevented me from being rational at that moment and put me at a significant disadvantage.

A CALL TO ACTION

This call to action might be challenging for some and might be a welcomed suggestion for others. Did you part ways with someone because you didn't see eye-to-eye on a matter? Was there someone whom, for a hundred other reasons, you loved, but for one reason you cast them aside? Reconnect and start again, don't be stubborn. Also, the next time you feel moved to lash out on an impulse, online or in person, don't! Take a deep breath and use that moment to think. Will this be something you will even remember a month later? Ask yourself if it's important at all. See God standing at your side, watching to see if you will follow His instruction to be slow to anger.

SCRIPTURES

- ❖ Proverbs 14:29
- ❖ Ecclesiastes 7:9
- ❖ Romans 12:18
- ❖ James 1:19-20

PRAYER

Father, thank You for the examples I have in Christ on how to handle situations involving those who attempt to anger me. Please soften my heart and open my mind so that I may be understanding and forgiving.

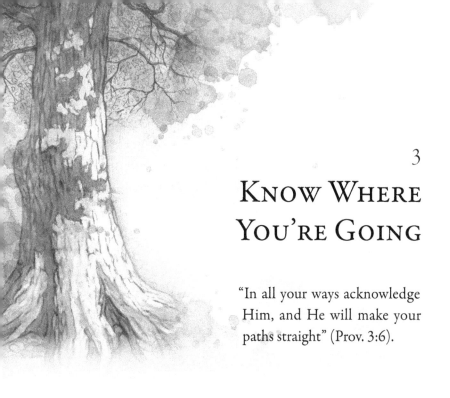

KNOW WHERE YOU'RE GOING

"In all your ways acknowledge Him, and He will make your paths straight" (Prov. 3:6).

When I was younger, my father was in the military and, for most of my childhood, he was stationed at Castle Air Force Base in Atwater, California. Base housing was not on the base but in town and separated into two groups. There was Old Base Housing and a newer group of homes, creatively called New Base Housing. A large field separated the two housing areas. During the day, cutting through the field was not a big deal, but it was another story at night. The field had no lighting, and it was completely undeveloped. On any given night, we avoided the field, but that was especially true on the creepiest night of the year, Halloween, or so one would think.

While I was perfectly content passing out candy and taking a share of my parent's purchase, my sister Leslie continued trick-or-treating well into her teens. She used Halloween as an opportunity to stay out late with her friends, which was exceptionally exciting when October 31st fell on a school night.

One warm Halloween evening, Leslie and her friends were enjoying their door-to-door festivities in New Base Housing. None of them stuck with the tradition of wearing costumes, but they did make sure they had their proper Halloween buckets; everyone, that is, except Naomi because her candy collector was a 'chitlin bucket.' As the night became darker, Leslie wanted to call it quits and head home to go through her stash, but Naomi wasn't quite ready to stop. She pointed towards the blackened field and yelled to the others, "Hey, let's go to Old Base Housing!"

"Nope! We aren't going in there. No way." Leslie replied.

Naomi tried to convince them to cross the dark field separating the neighborhoods, but they all refused. Finally, she said, "Ok, fine! I'll go by myself. Bye suckas!"

Naomi ran into the dark field with nothing more than a dim flashlight to assist her vision. Shortly after she disappeared, my sister heard a scream. Then, with the light of the full moon reflecting off its surface, Leslie and the others spied the 'chitlin bucket' flying end-over-end as it dispensed candy through the air. They later discovered that Naomi had tripped over a water hose and, as a result of the fall, she lost most of her candy. She tried to scoop up as many of her treats as she could from the ground in the dark, but it proved to be an exercise in futility. At that point, Naomi agreed with the others and decided to call it a night.

Leslie, Naomi, and the rest of their friends came to our house to go through the night's haul. I hadn't yet been told of Naomi's trip, so without knowing what happened when I looked into her bucket, I scratched my head and asked, "Who gave you dirt?"

Naomi learned that night what Leslie already knew; running through a dark, vacant field in the middle of the night, alone, even if you think you know the way, isn't a good idea.

It was Christmas 2015, and my husband and I were somewhat at a loss for what gift to get my parents. We, ultimately, decided on a gift card to Outback Steakhouse. We even personalized the gift card with a picture of them that was taken at our wedding. A few weeks after Christmas, I called my mother to ask her if they had used the gift card yet.

My mother said, "Baby, let me tell you what happened." Whenever my mother started a story with those words, I knew she was about to give me a good one.

"Your daddy and I were really looking forward to getting out and having a good time and enjoying our meal," she said with a slight giggle in her voice. "I got dressed up. You know the girl was lookin' cute, right? So, on our way there, I was telling your daddy how I was going to get a Bloomin' Onion, and he said he was going to get a steak. So, we get there, right. We ate our meal, and your daddy had his steak. It was good, baby!"

"Mama," I interrupted, "did you forget to bring the card with you?"

"No baby, we had the card. We made sure we had it before we left the house," she answered before continuing her story. "So, the waiter gave your daddy the check, and your daddy handed him the gift card. Then the waiter said, 'I'm sorry, sir, but I can't take this.' Your daddy said, 'Why not? It's an Outback card.' And the waiter said, 'I know sir, but this is Olive Garden.'"

I didn't know whether to laugh or cry. My first thought was how expensive it would be to care for them if they both went senile at the same time. Then I heard my mother explode in laughter, so I followed her lead and decided to laugh with her. After we finished laughing, I asked her to put Daddy on the phone. I asked, "Dad, with all of the talk about the Bloomin' Onion, didn't you think anything was weird when mom didn't get one?"

He replied, "No. I didn't think it was weird at all. It wasn't on the menu."

"Dad, how – just how – how did you end up at the wrong restaurant?"

"Baby, from the minute we got the gift card, I had in my mind *this* restaurant. I just thought this was the right restaurant, and I didn't even read. I was that convinced we were in the right place."

Christmas 2016, we gave them another gift card for Outback Steakhouse, but this time with a printout of Outback's location circled on a map!

THE LESSON

Running off unprepared into the dark or having an idea so fixed in our minds that we cannot see the signs letting us know we are in the wrong place have something in common. In both cases, we don't end up where we planned to be.

Ending up where we don't want to be can happen in our Christian walk. Sometimes we end up falling on our faces in the dark or at the wrong destination because we either didn't study God's word or blindly followed tradition. Each of us is supposed to know why we worship the way we worship and why we believe what we believe. Striving to gain that knowledge brings us into a relationship with God. He desires us to draw closer to Him. He wants a relationship with us, and He clears our way. We only need to seek Him and choose to do His will earnestly. He will light the darkness and clear the path for us. We don't have to run off on our own. He urges us to follow Him and wants us to do so willfully.

He never forces our decision to follow. If we keep our gaze focused upwards and on Him, we don't have to worry about tripping over anything that may lie ahead.

A CALL TO ACTION

Challenge yourself to know why you are on your path. You must know and understand why you believe what you believe. If asked, would you be able to support and defend your views using scripture? Can you confirm your stance using multiple scriptures? Using one of the following blank pages, write a belief you have that you have had to defend. It can be a belief about baptism, tithing, forgiveness, etc. Next, write every scripture you can find to support why you believe what you believe. Be sure to read the scripture in its entire context. Pray, study, seek and let Him light your path to the answer. Be open-minded, should the answer lead you in a direction that is different from your current beliefs.

SCRIPTURES

- ❖ Psalm 119:105
- ❖ Mark 7:5-13
- ❖ John 8:12
- ❖ 2 Timothy 2:15
- ❖ 1 Peter 3:15

PRAYER

Father, thank You for the confidence we have in You! Thank You for the reassurance we have in knowing that we do not need to worry when we give ourselves to You because You lead the way.

FUTURE JAILBIRD

"My son, do not reject the discipline of the Lord or loathe His reproof" (Prov. 3:11).

When it came to paying the price for misbehavior, my parents didn't deviate much from what was considered the norm. As we grew, the forms of punishment we encountered evolved but were still somewhat typical. We might have been banished to our rooms, unable to go outside, not allowed to hang out with friends, or maybe no television. There were a couple of times, though, where our parents did things a little differently.

Summer vacation was always rough in our house because the five of us would spend so much time together we'd get on each other's nerves. It's incredible how much we love each other today, considering how we fought with each other as kids when our parents weren't home. Our differences often didn't go past the arguing stage, but at times they would become physical. Leslie and I shared a room, so most of my arguments were naturally with her, and the same was true for Lucretia and Gina, as they shared a room.

On this summer morning, Lucretia and Gina's altercation began simple enough, with them shouting insults at each other. I can remember Gina telling Lucretia that her teeth were so yellow her tongue had to wear shades. It wasn't long after that when the arguing turned into a fight. Our mother came home on her lunch break and caught them, just as they were starting to wrestle with each other. She didn't ask what the fight was about because she didn't care. She just gave them the order to stop, and they did, at least while she was home. They knew Mom would leave again soon, so they were biding their time. Forty-five minutes later, Mom grabbed her keys and walked out of the door. The minute they believed she was gone, the fight started again. Mom wasn't stupid. She knew they were going to begin again, so she only pretended to leave. She came back into the house and told them both, "Get your coats and meet me in the car." Then she turned and walked out the door. The words themselves didn't seem concerning, but when you consider that Mom said it in a very emotionless, Terminator-like way and then turned to walk out of the house like Robo-Cop, it struck fear in our hearts. We knew she'd had it with these two. Leslie was worried and took it upon herself to sneak Gina a couple of dimes, so she could call from a payphone and let us know they were alright. (Told you Leslie should have been the oldest sister.)

About two hours later, Lucretia and Gina walked back into the house. As it turned out, what our mother had done was driven them a few miles away from our home to Avenue Two. Avenue Two was a stretch of road in Atwater that was fenced off on each side, and on the other side of the fences were cows. That entire road stunk like cow manure. Driving Avenue Two was an assault on the senses. She ordered the two to get out of the car, then rolled down her window and said, "Think about it while you're walking home." Then she drove off. Mom's creativity worked that day because they were no longer fighting when they walked into the house.

In raising our children, I incorporated a lot of what I learned from my parents. Standard discipline seemed to work well, but I, too, got creative one day to get a particular point across.

Jordan was in the fourth grade when I got a call from her school. They informed me that my daughter attempted to steal a pencil from the school book fair. My 'wanna-be' lawyer side kicked in, and I asked how they knew she was trying to steal the pencil. They told me they caught her holding it behind her back while trying to walk out of the library backward.

When she got home, I met her at the door and said, "So, you want to be a thief and go to jail someday?"

Jordan remained silent and stared at me. I told her to come inside, put her books away and change clothes. Once she'd done what I asked, I said, "Since you want to go to jail for stealing, I'm going to show you what it's like to be in jail. First, I want you to go into your brother's room and clean it. That's called community service." Jacob felt sorry for her and tried to help, but I wouldn't allow it.

After Jacob's room was clean, she reported back. I then said, "Ok, you know how you see people on the side of the road picking up trash? Those are people serving time in jail. Since that is the life you want to lead, go outside, get the shovel and the garbage bag, and clean up after the dog." She slowly walked outside and got to work. That wasn't something she was used to doing alone. She always split dog duty with her brother, and I knew not being able to complain about Jacob not doing his share of the work was killing her.

When she finished with cleaning detail, I told her to get ready for dinner. I yelled, "Chow time!" Jordan and Jake both came to the dining table. I handed Jacob his plate. On his dish were a delicious steak and baked potato, with all the toppings. I told Jordan to get a bowl and bring it to me where I was standing by the stove. She walked to the table, picked up a bowl, and brought it to me, where I had a pot cooking over low heat. I instructed her to hold the bowl with both hands and extend it out to me. She followed my instructions. I reached a serving spoon into the lukewarm pot and scooped up a heaping serving of pork-n-beans. Then, with a quick flip of my wrist, I plopped the beans into her bowl. Before this, I don't believe I had ever served the kids pork-n-beans. I gave her a slice of white bread, an apple, and a glass of milk and said, "While people in jail have to eat, they don't have to eat good."

After dinner, she went to her room and closed the door. I yelled, "Nope! The door stays open! People in jail don't have privacy!" I saw the door slowly open, but she stayed in her room. When the clock struck 9 p.m., I called for her to come to me so we could talk.

"So, what are your thoughts about today?" I asked.

"It was bad." She replied.

"Think you ever want to go to jail?"

With tears in her eyes, she looked at me and said, "No! Cause jail stinks!"

THE LESSON

We tend to think of discipline and punishment as the same, but there's a very critical difference between them. Punishment is imposing a negative consequence for an action, while discipline is training someone to obey a particular set of rules or code of behavior. I'll admit it's a fine line, but it's an important one.

We want to think that we're finished with discipline and punishment once we reach adulthood and liberate ourselves from our parents. But, as Christians, we aren't. Even as adults, being a Christian means we have an authority above us, who is still trying to discipline us to behave a certain way.

We must acknowledge the ultimate authority of God and understand that the Bible tells us He disciplines His children. In fact, we should exult in the discipline God gives, as that marks us as His true sons and daughters. He disciplines us so that we may share in His holiness. Isn't that what we want? When we are disobedient, we sin, and sin has consequences. These consequences can be a part of God's discipline for that sin, but they can also be an opportunity for growth and maturity.

Jesus never sinned, meaning He never had to be punished, but the writer of Hebrews tells us that Jesus did learn obedience. Should we be surprised that we, too, need to learn obedience?

A CALL TO ACTION

Do you feel as though you're currently going through hardship? Use the blank pages after this chapter to write what the difficulty is for you. If you know which of your actions led to what you're experiencing, write it down. You may or may not understand why you're facing your storm, and that's ok. If you do know, pray for God to help you change that part of your life. Also, use the pages to write what you think the Lord is trying to teach you. What are you learning from weathering the storm? When you look for the lesson and ask for God's help, there is a strong chance you will find He's telling you a lot more than, "Don't do that again."

SCRIPTURES

- ❖ Hebrews 5:8
- ❖ Hebrews 12:4-11

PRAYER

Thank You, Father, for loving me the way You do. Thank You for loving me enough to teach me the lessons I need to learn. Please help me to apply the knowledge gained from Your correction to every facet of my life.

5

SHOULD HAVE KNOWN

"Take heed, keep on the alert;
for you do not know when
the *appointed* time will come"
(Mark 13:33).

None of the Crawford kids enjoyed school. I know for a fact that I didn't. I did just enough to get the grades I needed to pass and keep my parents from getting phone calls from the school. I was no angel, that's for sure, and now that both of my children have graduated, I can admit to cheating on a couple of tests from time to time. One of the most memorable times came during 11th grade Spanish.

At the beginning of the year, our teacher issued the class workbooks and made us tear out the answer key. We all ripped the sheets out and passed them to the front of the class. She made sure she didn't miss a single student, as she collected each key and then locked them in a cabinet.

Two failed tests into the semester, I truly regretted signing up for that class. I knew what failing the course would mean to my GPA, and even though I was doing what I thought was necessary to prepare for upcoming exams, I was still floundering. I blamed Ms. Evans. She was a horrible teacher. I know all kids blame the teacher, but it's the truth because even the kids in class whose first language was Spanish were failing! They only took the class because they assumed it would be an easy A. Ms. Evans was an older lady, and she was starting to slip. She taught Spanish and German and would sometimes create sentences with words from both languages when she spoke in class. Leslie took her class two years after I did, and she was at least a few weeks into the course before she realized, "Guten Morgen, clase." was not how you say "Good morning, class." in Spanish.

As I sat in class, reading the assigned story for the day, I heard Ms. Evans say, "Continue reading, class, I'll be right back." Of course, the minute she walked out of the room, everyone stopped reading and began to talk about who would do what at lunch. I didn't participate in the lunch-time planning. I had other things on my mind, like how I was not going to fail this class. I ran to the window and watched as Ms. Evans turned the corner at the end of the walkway.

"Hey!" I yelled to the other students. Once I had their attention, I said, "I don't know about the rest of y'all, but I'm totally failing! Who else thinks we need the answer key if we're gonna make it through this class?"

They took a moment to grasp what I was asking, and then someone replied, "The key is in the top drawer of her desk!"

One of the easy A hopefuls yelled, "¡*Yo estoy contigo!*"

Thanks to Ms. Evans, I had no idea what that meant, but I assumed he was onboard. I told one of my classmates to keep watch out the window. A couple of the other students and I rushed to the desk. We found the key to the cabinet and took out one copy of the answer key. Ms. Evans was still nowhere in sight, so I took the time to tell the class that I'd make copies of the key and make sure they all got one, but that no one could continuously ace assignments. Everyone agreed, and we all passed the class.

That was my first time in a leadership role, and I must say I enjoyed it. Notice, I didn't say I was proud. I know that was not the correct way to handle that situation, but I share it only to say I knew my future if I didn't get a good grade.

My little brother, Wesley, was a bit different from me. He never seemed to be too concerned with our parents receiving calls from school. When he was in kindergarten, his teacher called our parents about a very pressing issue. After the conversation with his teacher, our parents sat down with my brother to discuss the call. Mom said, "Wesley, your teacher says you aren't turning in your homework."

Wesley threw his hands up, shook his head in dismay, and replied, "I know! I don't know why she keeps giving it to me. She knows I ain't gonna do it."

Being only five years old, Wesley had no idea about the importance of doing his homework. That was one of those moments when Mom and Dad had to make him leave the room, so he would not see them laugh, then bring him back to explain the fallacy of his ways.

Fast forward ten years. Wesley was now in high school and on the football team. I'm not much for sports, but even I could see the gift Wesley had. You name it, and he could play it. High school shined a light on Wesley's physical abilities, but it also shined a light on some of his old kindergarten ways.

Dad got a call from one of Wesley's teachers, telling him Wesley was not turning in his homework. It was deja vu. I was in the room when the call came, and I could see the anger on my dad's face. I thought to myself that Wesley should have known this phone call was coming. There was going to be no laughing this time. "Wesley!" my dad yelled.

Wesley ran into the room. "Yes, sir?"

"Boy, do you have any homework?"

I heard the question, and I knew my brother. I tried to coach him on what to say telepathically. *Tell him there's always homework. Tell him you're working on it. Tell him you finished it already.*

He didn't pick up on my brain waves. My brother wrinkled his brow as though he had to think about it, looked down at the ground for half a second, then looked back at our dad and replied, "I don't know." Even at 15 years old, he still wasn't prepared! Thankfully, as Wesley matured, he did finally catch on to the importance of doing homework.

To some people, even logical consequences can still come as a shock. In 1999, I was working for a heating and air conditioning company. There was a plumber who worked for the company; we'll call him Bob. At one time, Bob was a stellar employee, but as the years passed, his commitment to his work dwindled. I can recall making a *Top 10 Excuses Not Show Up to Work* list, based on Bob's *actual* excuses.

#9 was, "I have jury duty today."

#10 was, "I thought I had jury duty yesterday. I really have it today."

The time did come when the owner reached his tipping point. He summoned Bob on the Nokia radios we were using at the time. Since the owner was using a radio, I was able to hear both sides of the conversation. The owner pressed the button on the radio, and, in response, the radio made a beep sound. Then, he said, "Bob, are you there?"

<beep> "Yeah, I'm here." <beep>

<beep> "When will you be in the office? We need to talk." <beep>

<beep> "I'll be there in ten minutes." <beep>

Twenty minutes passed, no Bob.

<beep> "Bob, where are you?" <beep>

<beep> "Sorry, got stuck in traffic. I'm on my way. I'll be there in ten." <beep>

Twenty-five minutes passed, no Bob. By this time, the owner was furious. He angrily pressed the button on the radio,

<beep> "Fine, I wanted to say this to you in person, but since I don't know if you'll ever get here, I'll tell you on the radio. We have to talk about your job. You're late for your appointments. Our customers say you take too long to finish, and the jobs you touch are worse when you leave than they were when you got there. Am I going to have to bring in someone else?" <beep>

<beep> "Man, boss, I sure could use the help." <beep>

The owner stood speechless, staring at the radio. I was almost sorry I heard Bob's reply because I lost it. I was seven months pregnant with Jordan at the time, and I just knew laughing that hard could not have been good for my baby. Once I regained my composure, I couldn't help but wonder how in the world Bob could be so ignorant to the danger that was coming his way. The signs had been there for months.

THE LESSON

We have retirement plans, medical plans, and we pay extra to warranty products, never knowing for sure if we will need any of those precautions. One thing we know that is in our future, for sure, is the return of Christ. But even something that we know is coming can come in a manner that catches us off guard. Christ compares the destruction that will come with His return to labor pains. A pregnant woman knows for months labor is coming but with no knowledge of an exact time or date. The best she can do is prepare and be ready for that time, whenever it does finally arrive. When I was in Spanish class, I knew failing would complicate my future, so I took steps to prevent it. While cheating may have been good enough to pass a Spanish class, there is no cheating in our walk with the Lord. There are no shortcuts, and there is no bargaining. We can only prepare by obedience to His word.

Scripture also speaks of Christ's return as a thief in the night. It will catch the owners of the house entirely off guard. Like Wesley and Bob, there will be those focused on the present, ill-equipped for what is to come. A Christian's whole life should be in preparation for that day.

A CALL TO ACTION

Name one thing you currently do or partake in that you wouldn't do if you knew today was the day of the Lord's return. Once you've identified that action, start doing what you must to remove it from your life as you prepare for that day.

SCRIPTURES

- ❖ Matthew 24:36-44
- ❖ Matthew 25:1-13
- ❖ 1 Thessalonians 5:2-6
- ❖ Revelation 16:15
- ❖ Romans 14:11-12

PRAYER

Lord, I know the day is coming when my knee shall bow before You, and my tongue will praise You. Please guide me and strengthen me as I obey Your word in preparation for that day.

6

TAKE THE NEXT STEP

"For God has not given us a spirit of timidity, but of power and love and discipline" (2 Tim. 1:7).

Atwater High School was, and still is, the home of the Falcons! For years Atwater High offered a camp leadership opportunity for the students, and I have no idea what possessed me to sign up for it. Maybe I did it because my bff Melissa signed up too. Whatever the reason, I was not a camping kind of girl, and I knew this about myself. I got credit for taking part, but it wasn't worth it. I was miserable the entire time.

There were two problems with this gig. First, the campsite looked just like Camp Crystal Lake from *Friday the 13th*, and I knew Jason was going to kill us all! I was a kid who liked horror movies. I treated them like survival guides. When I watched a movie, I'd take mental notes; *if you ever find yourself in that situation, do not do that!*

That week, I put all of my horror movie survival skills into play. When I was in the bathroom, washing my hands, a brown icky substance dropped from the ceiling into the sink. Do you want to know what it was? Well, I can't tell you, because I never looked up. I saw the movie where the girl looked up, and the alien dropped from the ceiling onto her face! ET wasn't getting me! Plus, it wasn't lost on me that I'm black, and we never make it to the end, so I wasn't taking any chances. I can also remember hearing a strange noise outside, late one night after everyone had gone to bed. You already know I didn't investigate. My last words on earth were not going to be, "Hello? Anyone there?"

The second problem, the biggest one, the real one, was that it was cold. Since I lived in Atwater, where it was usually warm, I was totally unprepared for the colder fall weather. Yes, I said colder, *fall* weather. Don't be fooled! Certain places in California can get cold, and this camp's location was one of those places. I will admit, I was then, and still am, a big baby when it comes to what I consider perfect weather. If the temperature gets to 65 degrees, I'm wearing a jacket and a turtleneck. If it hits 50 degrees, I'm wearing a coat and looking for a different place to live.

One of the activities scheduled was a morning nature hike. I tried everything I could think of to get out of going; there simply was no escaping. I was, after all, a leader, and I had to do my part with the sixth graders who were on the trip. On the day of the hike, we began our trek at sunrise. I bundled up, as best I could, with the clothing I had. I think I put on everything I brought with me. If you are a fan of the show *Friends* and would like a visual, think of Joey when he put on everything Chandler owned. It wasn't enough. I was still freezing, especially my feet.

Something unexpected happened during that hike, though. Before starting the adventure, I had done nothing but dreaded it. I thought of how awful it would be and how much I didn't want to go. But, when the time came, and I knew I had no choice, I had a shift in my mindset. I told myself that I was one step closer to being warm again at the camp with each step I took. I would say, "Almost there." I didn't focus on how much further I had to go. I focused on how much closer I was.

In 2016, at age 45, having given birth twice and being happily married, I noticed I was gaining weight, and my clothes weren't fitting, as they once did. I told myself this was natural. I told myself being concerned with a growing waistline was vanity, and I wasn't going to be about that kind of life. I told myself my husband loved me no matter what, and that's all that mattered. I was lying to myself.

I wasn't unhappy with my appearance, but a thought did occur to me. While I may not be unhappy now, if I don't change my habits, my body and my health will continue to change and not in a good way. It so happened that same year, a stranger on Facebook saw a post I made about fitness and sent me a friend request. I don't usually accept requests from strangers, but I did that time. Her name was LaKeisha. She was a professional bodybuilder and has since become a dear friend. I told her I was struggling and I only wanted to lose five pounds. The truth was, I needed to lose much more, but I thought if I could lose five pounds, I'd be happy with seeing at least *some* progress. She immediately began giving me advice on how I could reach my goals. She told me to track my macros, stop doing so much cardio, and focus more on weight training, along with a host of other advice.

I implemented her suggestions, but I did have one serious struggle. I fought with the motivation to work out. I found excuses not to go. I would say it was too early or too late and, when I did go, I wouldn't push myself to get through the sets. I felt as though what I wanted was too difficult to obtain. When I thought about my goals, a list of reasons why I couldn't reach them would immediately come to mind.

Then I had this fantastic idea! I could ask John to help me. My husband was an athlete in high school and college, and he knew the fundamentals of working out. When I asked if he would go to the gym and coach me, he agreed without hesitation. I was so excited!

However, the man who went to the gym with me was not my husband! He looked and sounded like my husband, but that was not my husband! My husband would never yell at me or make a stink face at me. This guy, the imposter, did both of those things and so much more. He barked out commands like,

"You can go heavier than that!"

"You better not stop!"

"You said you were going to do twelve reps. I counted ten!"

"Mid-set break was over two seconds ago!"

"Do you feel like you're about to vomit? No? Go harder!"

"Why are you sitting down?"

"You better not pass out!"

"Stop being dizzy!"

"Your blood pressure is fine. Keep going!"

"No, I will not call an ambulance!"

During the workout, it dawned on me; he *was trying to kill me*. He wanted the life insurance money, and I gave him the perfect weapon—murder by workout! He would lie to the kids and tell them I died of natural causes, which the autopsy would support. I wanted to get my phone and at least tell Jacob and Jordan, one last time, that I loved them, but I knew if I reached for my phone during the workout, he'd lose it, so I endured.

An hour later, I was dripping with sweat and out of breath, but I was still alive! I didn't die. Instead, I learned I'd been cheating myself, and I was capable of so much more than I thought. The importance of that revelation was immense. Change didn't happen overnight, but it did happen. Eight weeks later, I was down 20 pounds and could see the definition in my body.

THE LESSON

We are so much stronger than we give ourselves credit. We cheat ourselves daily, with self-limiting beliefs that become self-fulfilling prophecies. God armed us to take on this world by giving us free will and the ability to make choices. The ability to choose to push through difficult circumstances is within each of us.

Too often, we mistake obstacles for roadblocks. When faced with something we know will be difficult, we must focus on reaching the goal, one step at a time, or risk the enormity of the situation paralyzing us. We have the power to make a way, even when we feel as though all hope is lost. Christians have the added benefit of knowing we endure nothing alone.

The Holy Spirit is our Helper. He's always there, urging us to keep going. However, He does more than give instruction. He gives us strength but the decision to take the next step is entirely up to us. When we act according to His will, He helps us and tells us not to worry. He tells us to have hope because we can do all things through Him!

A CALL TO ACTION

Grasp, for a moment, the comfort that comes with knowing we have God, the Almighty, as our strength! Using the blank pages in this chapter, write something you know you must do but, instead, have allowed mere obstacles to become roadblocks.

Write the obstacle, then write ten ways you can take the next step to go around it, over it, under it, or bust right through it! Don't stop until you hit ten ways. Even if they seem silly, write them down anyway. The magic number is ten because it will force you to think outside the box. If the answer were simple, you would have done it already.

After you have your list, pray for God's help, then go for it! Take action before negative self-talk has a chance to steal your joy. Then keep stepping and moving forward!

SCRIPTURES

- ❖ 1 Chronicles 16:10-11
- ❖ Isaiah 40:28-31
- ❖ Philippians 4:13

PRAYER

Lord, thank You for always being there, willing to help me, and for being my strength. Please, never let me grow weary of doing what You call me to do. Lord, allow me to develop a positive mindset in all that I do. I know, with You, all things are possible.

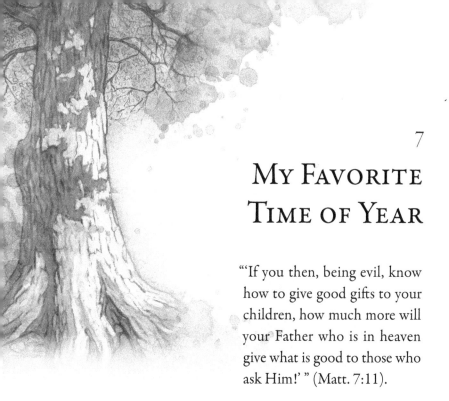

7

My Favorite Time of Year

"'If you then, being evil, know how to give good gifts to your children, how much more will your Father who is in heaven give what is good to those who ask Him!'" (Matt. 7:11).

Christmas has always been my favorite time of year. I know many people say the same, but I think I might be next level. As a child, I loved it for all the same reasons most children do; the presents! My parents always did their best to make sure there were plenty of gifts under our Christmas tree.

Every year, starting in October, when toy ads would overrun the commercials between cartoons, Leslie, Lucretia, and I would watch while trying to figure out what we were going to ask Santa to bring us. We had this rule, the first one to yell, "I want that!" would be the one Santa would bring that toy. Somehow, Santa would just know who shouted it first. Christmas was that one day when anything was possible. That thing you longed for all year could magically show up under the tree! I always thought big when thinking of Santa.

Our parents thoroughly enjoyed our anticipation on Christmas Eve and our joy on Christmas morning. One year, they woke us

45

"after Santa left" so that we could rush to the window and catch a glimpse of him as he rode out of sight.

"Wake up! He just left! Come look out the window, or you're going to miss him!"

Tangled in the blankets but trying to hurry, I fell out of bed. Hitting the floor like that on any other morning may have made me cry, but not Christmas morning. No time for tears, because Santa was getting away and I had to see him! I pushed five-year-old Leslie out of the way and ran to the window, where our parents were holding the curtain back for us to see. I put my face to the cold glass, looked up into the dark sky, and there he was! I saw Rudolph's nose and everything! It wasn't just me either, because when Leslie did finally reach the window, she looked out and yelled, "I see him!"

When I think back, I'm pretty sure we were looking in different directions.

As special as Christmas was in the Crawford house, I'm the only one of my siblings who held on to the magic. All of us celebrate Christmas, but I'm the only one who takes pictures of trees once they go on sale in September and then texts those pictures to the others, with the message, "I'm so happy right now." Last November, in our Crawford siblings group chat, a conversation concerning COVID-19 began about which vitamins to take. I used the opportunity to text, "In the midst of all this, please don't forget, they're playing Christmas carols on the radio." Leslie dropped me from the group.

It should come as no surprise that I wanted my children to love Christmas as much as I did. Each year we would make cookies, watch

Frosty and Rudolph and then, once the kids were in bed, I would watch my favorite Christmas movie, *Die Hard*! I kept the dream of Santa alive for them, as long as I possibly could. I even went as far as to have a friend dress up as Santa and visit our house when Jordan began to doubt, at age four. Whenever we went shopping, I would pay close attention, so I could notice which toys made their eyes light up. Then, on Black Friday, I'd go out to the stores, prepared to fight to the death, if I had to, to get those toys. Oh, great times!

When Jacob turned eight, he asked me to tell him the truth about Santa, and I realized I needed to be honest with him. He was old enough to know the truth, and I knew I couldn't continue with the fantasy. So, I looked him in the eye, braced myself, and then I pretended I didn't hear what he'd asked and offered him some cookies. Sadly, diversion only bought me a couple of more days. I fessed up and admitted that his father and I were Santa, but I told him he needed to continue to go along with pretending to believe for the sake of his little sister. He agreed to continue. However, there was one significant change.

Each year I would have the kids write out their Christmas list. I loved watching the effort that went into trying to remember the names of toys they had seen in commercials and treasured their notes to Santa, written in that unmistakable child-like script. Once Jacob found out there was no Santa, he stopped writing the list. I knew not to expect him to write a letter, but I still encouraged him to write a list of the things he would like to appear under the tree for Christmas. Nope! Nothing!

He would say, "Whatever you want to get me, Mama, is fine."

I wanted a list. That list kept me from wasting time and money. Without that list, I spent hours in toy stores looking for presents I hoped would make Jacob happy. I'd look at a toy and then its price tag and think, "I'm not spending all this money without knowing if he'll even like it. This boy better not get mad when he finds Capri-Sun under the tree!"

I knew why the lists stopped. Even at eight, Jacob had some understanding of money and knew we were by no means wealthy. He didn't want to ask us to spend money on gifts for him. What Jacob didn't understand was how much I loved having a list. While I enjoyed shopping for him, I relished, even more, knowing how excited he would be when he opened a gift for which he'd been asking.

Jacob and Jordan are adults now, and the love of Christmas never really filtered down to them like I hoped it would. Jordan claims Halloween is her favorite time of year. I still love Christmas just as much as I always have, and John is a massive fan of the holiday as well. I may have failed with Jacob and Jordan, but I will do better with our grandchildren!

THE LESSON

God is not Santa Claus, but He wants us to share our heart's desires with Him, not just one day out of the year but every day! Coming to Him, even with requests, is a part of our relationship with Him. He is there, ready, willing, and a lot more than able. What's essential in presenting our requests to God is they mustn't be selfish, and they must be in accordance with His will.

Jabez prayed to God to bless him, and we can do the same. He wants to bless us. How often do we rob God of the delight of seeing our eyes light up as we ask Him for something that would bring us happiness? Before my son knew there was no Santa, he would write his list with such enthusiasm, and I cherished it. Even knowing I wouldn't get him everything on his list, I still wanted to know what he wanted. God wants to see the joy and anticipation in us that can only come from those who have complete faith in Him. He wants us to be thrilled to see what He is going to do with our list.

Imagine how pleased God must become when He sees a list, where our requests fall in line with His will for us. It's a fine line, but God wants for us what we want for us when what we want for us is what He wants for us! (Yeah, I know you probably had to read that last sentence twice, but it does make sense.) We can, and do, restrain God, either by not asking at all, by asking with selfish motives, or by not asking with faith that believes nothing is too great for Him. Be sure your requests are in accordance with His will, then pray often, pray hard, and pray big and small.

A CALL TO ACTION

Think of what you need to be the servant He would have you to be. Do you need more strength, more energy, more self-discipline? Do you need more wisdom? More opportunities? Do you need to know what your gift is? Do you need to know what His will is for you? Use the blank pages of this chapter to make a list and then present it to God with joy and anticipation!

SCRIPTURES

- ❖ 1 Chronicles 4:10
- ❖ Philippians 4:6-7
- ❖ James 4:2-3
- ❖ 1 John 5:14

PRAYER

Father, thank You for Your willingness to bless me with my heart's desires. My heart desires You, Lord, and Your will for me. As I present my requests to You, Father, I pray that my heart is in an unselfish place, and as You bless me, help me to bless someone else.

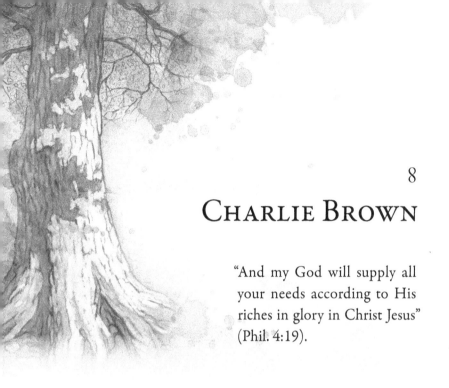

8

CHARLIE BROWN

"And my God will supply all
your needs according to His
riches in glory in Christ Jesus"
(Phil. 4:19).

I n January 2017, after leaving my job of 14 years, I found myself
working for another locally owned company in Tucson. My salary
was ok, and I had a great manager, but I began to feel unfulfilled in
my job after the first year. My friend, Rashundra, worked there, and
she, too, wanted a different opportunity. Rashundra was a woman
of faith and one of my closest friends, so it made total sense to ask
her if she wanted to pray together about our situations.

She was more proactive than me when it came to taking steps
to find another job. She even had interviews during the first couple
of weeks of our prayer sessions. It didn't take long after we started
praying together for God to move. It was the end of August 2018,
and Rashundra told me she had received a call from a company at
which she hadn't applied. They had her information and wanted
to talk with her about an opportunity. God was moving for sure!
By the first week of September, they made her an offer. I was so

happy for her but a little envious at the same time. I wanted out as well, and then the Lord answered my prayers too! The same week Rashundra was made an offer, so was I. My offer was a severance package; I got fired.

I think they were expecting to see me shed tears when they delivered the news of my termination. I didn't. I refused to shed even one tear. They told me the company would continue to pay me until the end of the year. That meant I had four months to find another job before I would be without a paycheck.

I immediately began my job search. The first position for which I applied was as an Office Administrator at a law firm. This job paid more money than I've ever made in my life. The job also came with a lot more responsibility and required skillsets I had yet to achieve. I was scared to death, but I prayed about it and went for it anyway. I thought of what that check could do for my family, and I prayed hard. Thanks to a personal connection, I was invited to interview. I know I impressed everyone because I made it to the second round of interviews. The second interview is where the hope for this position ended. The partners of the firm decided to offer the job to someone else. I questioned my faith and blamed myself for the Lord not answering my prayer. I told myself that I wavered too much. I promised next time I would not doubt. I would have faith.

My next opportunity came two weeks later when I interviewed for an Office Manager position. By this time, it was late October. I only had two more months before I'd be without a paycheck, and offers were not flooding in. Once again, I did exceptionally well in the first interview, and they invited me back to the final round. In the second round, I also did well. I know, because they told me so before I left. They said they would inform me of their decision within a couple of days. This position, I felt, was a perfect fit for me, much better than the one at the law firm. I prayed my job search was over. I kept reminding myself of James 1:6, "But he must ask in faith without any doubting, for the one who doubts is like the surf of the sea, driven and tossed by the wind."

I knew the date of when to expect their decision. When that morning arrived, I headed to the gym to start my day with a workout. While on my way, I called my husband to tell him I was no longer worried. I told him I knew this job would be mine and that I was wrong for not praying as though I had already received it. Within a minute after hanging up with my husband, my phone rang. It was them; I didn't get the job.

I parked my car, and that is when I allowed myself to cry. The tremendous wave of disappointment that came over me was somewhat paralyzing. I had no other job interviews and only became dismayed when searching job sites and seeing all the jobs I felt I wasn't qualified to get. I felt low, and I felt useless. I felt like I'd made all the wrong decisions in life, but mostly, I felt betrayed. I called Kelly, another Christian confidant of mine, to tell her what happened. I was nervous to say what I was thinking out loud, but I asked anyway, "Why are we told to pray as though we've already received?" I told her I felt like Charlie Brown.

By that, I was referring to Charlie Brown from the comics and his attempt to kick a football that Lucy always swears she'll keep upright for him. She can always convince Charlie Brown of how wonderful he will feel once he kicks that ball and how he can trust her to hold it. Each time she successfully lures him with her promises. Without fail, he speeds toward the football, confident he will experience the satisfaction of kicking it to the moon. Of course, the second before he swings his foot to kick the ball, she yanks it away, and he slams on his back to the ground. That's how I felt. I ran for the football and had slammed hard.

In November, two months after losing my job and after two rejections, I received a call to interview for a position for which I hadn't applied. The employer found me on LinkedIn. The position was a six-month contract job working for Intuit. Getting the contract job wouldn't make me an Intuit employee, but I would be working at their office and doing work for them. I interviewed and got the contract position. I didn't want a job that came with an expiration date, but I wasn't exactly in a place where I could afford to reject opportunities.

As a contractor, I still went through the same orientation process as official Intuit employees. I was floored! I mean, forget the half-basketball court or that you could eat breakfast and lunch at the cafeteria for under $7 total; it was how the company treated their employees that got my attention. The people who worked there were genuinely happy. The company adopted a philosophy that stated they wanted to enable their talented employees to do the best work of their lives. Even on the outside looking in, it was easy to see the strides Intuit took to create a pleasant and productive work environment. I had to find a way to become a member of the Intuit team.

The month before my contract was to end, I interviewed for two jobs at Intuit. I also interviewed for a job outside of Intuit and was offered that position. I accepted the outside work and had a start date set for the week after my contract ended. It was my Plan B, just in case I wasn't offered either of the positions with Intuit. As it turned out, I didn't need Plan B; I was offered both jobs at Intuit! When I received the call from the recruiter with the second offer, her first words to me were, "You have a decision to make."

I went from being down in the dumps, feeling useless, to having three job offers!

God hadn't answered my prayer by saying no. God knew the level of stress the law firm would have placed on my life. I met the woman they hired, and she didn't have the job for even a year before deciding it was too much. God also considered things I hadn't. I'm high cancer risk, and praying for a position with tremendous benefits never factored into my prayers. Even though I may not have been thinking about benefits, God was. Intuit offered benefits that went above and beyond, saving my husband and me thousands on medical bills. God also considered what I couldn't possibly have known. For example, how could I have known on that November morning in 2018, as I sat in a parking lot crying over a job I didn't get, that there was a virus on its way, and it was going to turn the whole world upside down in just a little over a year.

I don't believe the job I cried over survived the COVID-19 lockdowns. Intuit, however, was able to turn on a dime with work-from-home changes. They flexed for their employees, during a tumultuous year, by giving extra vacation days, adding two additional weeks to our sick days in case we became ill or needed to take care of someone who was, and they helped provide office furniture for our home offices. What I thought was a "No" from God was actually an "I got you."

THE LESSON

You may have noticed there was no Crawford Kids part of my life for this lesson. As a child, nothing I experienced could have prepared me for the stress of losing a job. As a child, you don't have years behind you to reflect upon and wish you'd made better choices. This lesson comes from growth, and it comes when life holds your faith to the fire. I know I had my low moment, but I've always known that God is nothing like Lucy. He's not waiting to rip the football away as soon as we establish trust in Him.

The Bible tells us that His ways are not our ways, and God sees things we cannot see. I wrongly interpreted the employment rejections as a "No" to my prayers when, in fact, God knew my needs, as well as the future. I hadn't thought of any other way God might provide, outside of how I wanted Him to provide. I was praying for my will, which was to have *that* Office Manager job, instead of praying for God's will for me, which, turns out, was all about protecting me. When I really think about it, I didn't want that Office Manager job; I wanted what I felt that job would provide; a paycheck, stability, a sense of worth. God gave me exactly what I needed and so much more. He gave it to me by denying me what I asked.

We are so narrow in our thinking! Too often, we look at not getting what we ask as a "No" from God, instead of seeing it as, "I have something better in mind for you." If I only could have remembered to lean on God and trust Him, I would not have wasted so much of my time in tears and confusion. Faith is like a muscle, and it becomes more powerful the more we put it to use. And when our faith is strong, we can move mountains.

A CALL TO ACTION

Are you willing to trust God and allow Him to provide for you in the way *He* sees as best? Pray for what you truly want and need, not for how you think God should give it to you. Our imagination is limited, but God's is not! He can answer your prayers in ways that may blow your mind!

SCRIPTURES

- ❖ Isaiah 55:8-9
- ❖ Matthew 6:7-13
- ❖ Mark 11:22-24
- ❖ Ephesians 3:20-21
- ❖ Hebrews 11:6

PRAYER

God, help me pray as Christ did, that all things I ask be granted only if in accordance with Your will. Please help me to trust You fully. You see 10,000 steps beyond what I could ever hope to consider. So, when something doesn't go according to my plan, help me not to wallow in defeat but, instead, praise You and remain hopeful for what is yet to come.

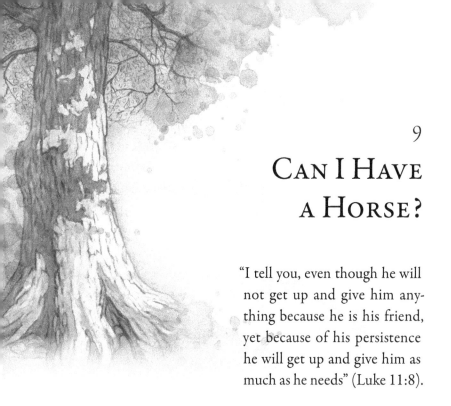

9

CAN I HAVE
A HORSE?

"I tell you, even though he will
not get up and give him anything because he is his friend,
yet because of his persistence
he will get up and give him as
much as he needs" (Luke 11:8).

A ll children must ask permission for things they would like to
do from time to time. Asking my mother for permission was
rough. I hated how my mom would tell us no. It was hardly ever a
simple, no. We would ask a question, and she'd reply with a question, one to which she knew the answer would be no. Our no to her
question also served as her no to our question.

"Mom, can I go to the football game?"

"Is my kitchen clean?"

"Mom, can I go to a sleepover at Melissa's?"

"Can you take Gina?"

And, of course, the universal favorite,

"Mom, can we go to McDonald's?"

"You got McDonald's money?"

I started to avoid asking anything if I thought the answer to my question would be no because if she replied by, let's say, asking if the bathroom was clean, I'd have to go clean the bathroom.

I can remember wanting a slice of cake that my mother had made earlier in the day. I'd already had some, and there was no doubt in my mind that if I asked my mother for more, she was going to ask something crazy like was the driveway swept. So, I went to my brother, the youngest and the only boy, so, Mom's favorite son. He was adorable and still had that sweet way of mispronouncing words. I went to Wesley and asked, "Wes, do you want some cake?"

Wesley had not been thinking about cake before being asked if he wanted any. He was too busy enjoying privacy in his bedroom, something I never had, but I'm not bitter or anything. He looked at me and said, "Yes."

He was so cute, and innocent, and trusting. I almost feel bad for those times I tricked him into trading me a quarter for two pennies by telling him I'd give him two monies for his one money. But hey, that's what big sisters do, and at that moment, big sister wanted cake. I told him, "If you want cake, you have to ask Mom for it first."

Wesley got up and proceeded to walk towards our parent's room. Before he opened the door to go in, I called to him and said, "Wes, when you ask, be sure to say, can me and Silvia have some cake!"

My indirect, complicated way of handling things was never the approach taken by my little girl; not even close. Jordan lives by a different motto. She never asked a question with a pre-determined answer in mind. Instead, Jordan asked and then waited for the reply. If there was a glimmer of hope for a yes, and I mean a glimmer, she would go for it. I can describe it best by referring to the movie, *Dumb and Dumber*. There is a scene when Lloyd asks Mary, a woman he likes, "What are my chances?"

"Not good." she replies.

"Like one in 100?"

"More like one in a million."

"Sooooooo, you're telling me there's a chance!" he says with a smile.

That's my Jordan! If there is a chance, no matter how slim, she is going to ask. She once asked us for a horse. I know that's a common ask, but she wasn't three or four years old, she was nine, and she had some idea of what it took to take care of a horse. I know she knew it couldn't live in our garage. We, of course, told her she could not have a horse. I couldn't understand why she would even ask. But she didn't ask just the once; Jordan asked again and again.

I realize now that she asked so often because I never explained why the answer was no, nor did I tell her to stop. Not explaining to Jordan why she couldn't have a horse only led to her asking me repeatedly. Her constant ask did do one thing. It let me know that her desire to have a horse in her life was not fleeting. So, when I became friends with a couple who owned horses, I asked them if they wouldn't mind allowing Jordan to do some work with their animals. Jordan was able to ride the horses, but she also had to help with the less than glamorous chore of picking up after them. As you can imagine, the requests for a horse of her own soon stopped after that experience.

Then there was the cruise.

"Mom, can we go on a cruise?"

"No."

"Can I ask why?" Yes, I let her know it was ok to ask for a reason.

"Because we can't afford to take you and Jacob on a cruise."

That was the end of the conversation. A few days later, links started showing up in my email box. "Book now! Amazing rates on our staterooms!" She became a fifth-grade travel agent. Every time she found a better deal than the last one I said no to, she would ask me again, fully believing that this new deal would be the one to which I would say yes. Finally, I told her the answer was no and to stop asking. I wondered why I hadn't told her to stop asking sooner.

Then, one day, I saw an ad. I learned we could all go on a three-day Disney cruise to the Bahamas for a little under $2,000. Without hesitation, I booked the tickets. I was super excited to do so and absolutely couldn't wait to share the news with Jordan. If she had only asked me once or twice, I would have dismissed the ad entirely. Her repeated plea also had another unintentional effect. She showed me she believed me when I said cost was the only real factor. She believed one hundred percent that we would take her on a cruise if we could afford it.

THE LESSON

My parents always did whatever they could, whenever they could, for us. It was silly of me to be timid about asking for things I wanted. How much did I deny myself because I didn't ask?

God isn't like an earthly parent. He doesn't get tired of hearing us ask. We aren't to be afraid to come to Him with our requests, nor are we to stop at just asking once! Jordan never stopped asking because she never stopped believing there was a way. How often do we stop asking because we lose faith? No matter how big, small, significant, or insignificant we think our requests may be, we are to ask, and ask, and ask.

A CALL TO ACTION

Using one of the blank pages in this chapter, write down ten desires of your heart. They can be big things, little things, material things, or intangible things. God wants to hear it all but start by writing down ten. Pray continuously over what you've written. Be sure to examine your heart when praying over these things because you know God will.

SCRIPTURES

- ❖ Psalm 5:3
- ❖ Luke 11:5-10
- ❖ Luke 18:1-8
- ❖ 1 John 5:14-15

PRAYER

Father, I will present my desires to You with new hope, knowing that You are able. Please help my desires to align with Your will so that I may pray without reservation.

10

Jumping on the Couch

"And just as they did not see fit to acknowledge God any longer, God gave them over to a depraved mind, to do those things which are not proper" (Rom. 1:28).

I can't count the number of times growing up when I would leave something in the fridge, in hopes of having it as a snack when I got home, only to find one of my sisters or my brother had beaten me to it. Even when I tried to hide it, they were still able to find it. No one in the house could ever eat in peace. There would always be someone there to ask for a bite or someone who would eat it when you weren't looking. Every member of the family cherished those moments when we could eat something without being bothered.

The trouble we would go through to ensure we could eat whatever it was in its entirety knew no bounds. My father went on a quest for an ice cream his children wouldn't touch, and he found it the day he brought home butter pecan. My mom's cottage cheese was always safe. Wesley got creative. Wesley would purposefully cough over whatever he was eating. He once thought it would be funny to play that game with his Snickers bar. He coughed over it, then extended it to me and asked, "Want some?"

I coughed over it too and said, "No, thank you."

One day, Lucretia and I made a stop at our favorite sandwich shop in Atwater, Happy Sub, where she ordered a foot-long sandwich. We placed our order in the drive-thru, and our next stop was home, which was approximately seven minutes away. I left my sandwich in the bag, with the intent to eat it once we arrived home. Lucretia, however, didn't want to take any chances. No one at the house would even have the opportunity to ask for a piece of her sandwich. She unwrapped the sandwich and feverishly began eating. I told her to slow down, or she was going to make herself sick. I even told her she was going to choke. My words landed on deaf ears. The entire ride home, I kept telling her that was too much food to be eaten that quickly. She didn't slow down at all and was barely chewing.

Seven minutes after we left the sandwich shop, we were home, and she had utterly devoured her sandwich. Eight minutes after we left the sandwich shop, Lucretia threw up. I know she would rather have shared her sandwich than lived through the teasing that followed. None of us were going to just let it go. As siblings, it was our duty to remind Lucretia of the incident every chance we got. Sometimes we would act like we were going to throw up after eating a sandwich, and other times we would give her a footlong, a stopwatch, and a pail, then dare her to beat her personal best.

I never forgot how hard I tried to get her to do something for her own good and how determined she was not to listen.

Years later, I thought of my warnings to Lucretia as I found myself repeatedly telling Jacob, when he was a toddler, to stop jumping on the couch. Usually, Jacob would do what I told him, but there were times when he would get something in his head, and there was no deterring him from it with mere words. He had a favorite toy, and I couldn't convince him to play with anything else. He had a favorite movie, and when I got tired of hearing the same movie over and over, my efforts to get him to watch something else were utterly wasted. Getting him to eat different foods was an especially unique challenge. I once attempted to get him to eat a peanut butter and jelly sandwich. He'd never had one, and I believed he would love it if he just tried it.

"Taste this, honey." I said.

"Don't wanna yike it." was his reply as he shook his head.

After several attempts, I was finally able to coax him into taking a bite. He chewed it a couple of times, then gave a disapproving look and ran away. I accepted defeat and decided to finish the sandwich myself. I put the plate down, left the dining room, and went into the kitchen to get a glass of milk. Jacob was nowhere to be found upon my return, but I did notice he had attempted to destroy the evil he felt lurked in a PB&J sandwich. He had stabbed it with an ink pen and a crochet hook.

Unfortunately, one of the things Jacob found joy in was jumping on the couch, and it was one of the activities he had gotten stuck in his head. I physically caught him in my arms, preventing his fall more than once, and he interpreted it as some kind of game. I would repeatedly tell him that he would get hurt, but he had no fundamental concept of what that meant. I tried using words like *owie*, *ouchy*, and *boo-boo* to get the point across. Just like Lucretia with the sandwich, he wouldn't heed my warnings and, just like Lucretia, he was only going to learn this lesson the hard way.

After days of catching him, I decided to allow him to learn this lesson. I had to let him fall. I first made sure the coffee table and anything else that could injure him was out of the way. Then I sat down and watched as he climbed onto the couch. Once he was standing, he began to jump. I felt like the most horrible mother in the whole world, but I knew the day would come when he would fall, and better that he did it while I was there watching, with the surroundings prepared. Twenty seconds into his joyous romp, it happened. One of his precious little feet missed its intended spot on the couch, and he fell. I quickly moved to his side on the floor as he began to cry.

I never again had to tell him not to jump on the couch, but I did have to ask him to quit stabbing my PB& J sandwiches.

THE LESSON

Why are we determined to learn things the hard way? God's Word warns us of pitfalls in life. Our selfish nature or desire to do what makes us feel good deafens us to these warnings. I know there have been times in my life, too many sadly, where God had to let me fall for me to learn my lesson. We are like Adam and Eve; they knew God's instructions but ignored the warning. If we choose to ignore God's warning, if we choose to disobey, we must also accept the fact that He will stand back and eventually permit us to fall.

He wants to catch us, but sometimes being caught is what prevents us from learning the lesson. It's not His desire that any of us should get hurt, but if we are determined to keep jumping on the couch, God will allow us to suffer the consequences of our defiance. The good news is God knows we are going to fall, and much like the father in the Parable of the Lost Son, more commonly known as The Prodigal Son, He will be there for us when we repent and return to Him.

A CALL TO ACTION

Are there any areas in your life where you can hear The Spirit telling you to stop or change your ways? Are you ignoring Him? Are you refusing to heed warnings for selfish reasons? Take a moment to think of the direction in which your actions are taking you.

If you don't feel strong enough to stop the behavior, reach out for help. Find support from loved ones and fellow Christians. Never forget to pray. God will not stand by and simply watch if you make an effort to acknowledge His presence and ask for His help.

SCRIPTURES

❖ Genesis 2:16-17
❖ Proverbs 1:29-31
❖ Luke 15:11-32

PRAYER

Lord, You are patient and merciful. You stand back and allow me to make my own choices, even when that choice is to ignore Your voice. Help me to listen to Your warnings and obey Your word.

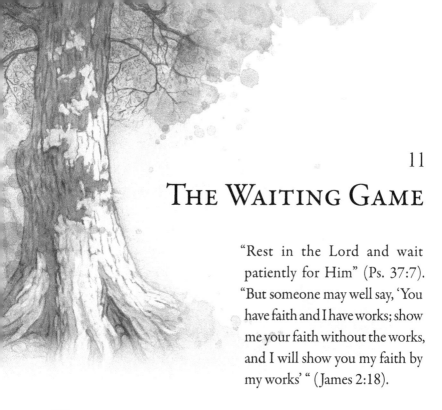

11

THE WAITING GAME

"Rest in the Lord and wait
patiently for Him" (Ps. 37:7).
"But someone may well say, 'You
have faith and I have works; show
me your faith without the works,
and I will show you my faith by
my works' " (James 2:18).

One task that always fell to our mother was taking care of her
daughter's hair. That was something our father only did in
our mother's absence, and, even then, we would try to wait for Mom
if we could. Dad's attempt at ponytails left much to be desired.

Our mother was a ninja with a hot comb and a master with a
spring-handled, non-electric curling iron. In the mid to late '70s,
a hot comb, curling iron, and hair grease were tools of the trade
for styling a black girl's hair. A hot comb was a brass comb with a
wooden handle. Mom would put the comb on the eye of the stove to
let it become searing hot. Once the comb was hot enough, she'd part
a section of our hair and slowly run the comb from root to end, then
repeat. She would move slowly, going one section at a time. Our
mom used this technique to make our tightly wound coils extremely
straight. The worst part of the process was when Mom would have
to get the hairline's edges and *the kitchen*. The kitchen was what we
called the hair at the nape of the neck, but don't ask me why.

Somehow and someway we'd always get burned. It never failed. Mom was cautious, as were we, but it didn't matter. We did everything we could think of to avoid getting burned. We'd hold our ears down so that she could get to the hairline on the sides of our heads, and we'd stop chewing if we had gum in our mouths because we didn't want our temples moving. But no matter what, we never escaped without getting at least one burn. This activity could take up an entire Saturday afternoon for my mother, who had to perform this process on four heads. Straightening our hair required patience, but that's not to say my mother was a patient woman.

Although my brother's hair was our father's responsibility, there were those times when Mom thought she could do just as good a job with Wesley as Dad. I can remember her first attempt to cut Wesley's hair with electric clippers. She told Wes to have a seat in the kitchen in the chair she had prepared for him using the Yellow Pages as a booster seat. Once Wes was seated, she placed a towel around his neck. Glowing with confidence, she picked up the clippers. She instructed Wes to lower his head as she turned them on. I saw her move the clippers down to the back of my brother's head. Then I heard the clippers make a short-lived cumbersome buzz sound, and then I saw a clump of hair fall to the floor. I looked at my mother, who was staring at the back of my brother's head. As she stared, her eyes widened to the size of silver dollars. Without a word, she turned the clippers off, removed the towel from around his neck, helped him down from the chair, then said, "Baby, go get your daddy."

She was done with clippers, but Wesley's hair adventures were far from over.

In the early 80s, waves and Jheri Curls were all the rage, and my mother asked my dad to put waves in eight-year-old Wesley's hair. Dad agreed, but after a few days of waiting for Dad to do it, Mom became impatient and decided to take matters into her own hands. She armed herself with Dax Pomade and a brush and went to work. Like my dad had no business doing ponytails, my mother had no business trying to do waves. She made a comedy of errors, the first of which was not realizing Wesley's hair was too long for waves. With the best of intentions, she brushed the pomade in Wesley's hair one morning before school, and once she was happy with the results, she sent him on his way.

On the day Mom attempted waves, I was the first to arrive home, so I was there when Wesley and Gina walked in the door after school. I saw that Wesley's hair had somehow sectioned itself off, and instead of looking like waves, he had what looked like rocks sitting on his head. His hair looked like something resembling a desert landscape. I instantly started laughing. I couldn't help myself. The laughter was spontaneous and involuntary, and it just came out.

When Leslie and Lucretia got home, their reaction was the same as mine. Leslie attempted to make Wesley feel better by saying, "It doesn't look that bad, Wes." (Told you she should have been the oldest sister.)

Mom arrived home before Dad and, of course, when she saw Wesley, she didn't laugh. She knew she was responsible, so she attempted to console Wes, who, by this time, was in tears. Then Dad came home. He immediately ordered all of us to stop laughing! My father didn't hold back on us, not at all. He let us know how wrong we were for laughing at our little brother and even expressed his frustration with our mom. He let her know never to attempt anything like that with Wesley's hair, ever again! Dad successfully put an end to all the laughter. He was Wesley's hero. He turned to Wesley and said, "Don't worry, son, I'll fix your hair."

Wesley stopped crying and said, "Thanks, Daddy."

"It's ok, son. I'm going to go change out of my uniform, and then I'll cut your hair." Dad hugged Wesley and then said, "I'll be right back."

I was in my parent's room, speaking to my mother, when my father came into the room loudly speaking to Wesley over his shoulder, "It'll be alright, son. I'm just going to change out of my uniform. Daddy will fix it. Love you."

Then dad closed the door and fell to his knees. Laughing uncontrollably, he looked at us and said, "Did you see that boy's head?"

In my professional career, the longest stint of time I've spent with any company is 14 years. It should have been 12. I knew every aspect of my job, and I was extremely comfortable in my position, but my job search should have begun the day HR informed me that my position had capped out on salary. They told me I would no longer receive pay increases; instead, I would receive a bonus (which I knew the government would tax to death). I was upset, and my husband advised me to quit. Foolishly, I didn't. I made up several excuses to stay, despite John and common sense telling me otherwise. I should have seen that the salary cap was their way of saying they no longer appreciated me.

As time passed, I became more miserable. As miserable as I was, though, I still didn't begin searching for a new job. The uncertainty of starting something new terrified me, and I had myself convinced, if I weren't meant to be employed there any longer, God would make sure I had no fear or reservation about leaving. The final straw came when the company hired a new manager, and he informed us that going to the bathroom would be logged as taking a break. Upon hearing that news, I immediately began my search for something new. It took only two weeks to find my next job.

THE LESSON

These experiences represent two sides of the same coin, and they both boil down to faith. There is a difference between being patient in faith and blaming complacency on faith. My mother had neither the skills nor the knowledge to do what she wanted, and her lack of patience led to an undesired outcome. On the other hand, my lack of action caused me to be in a bad situation far longer than I should have been. I claimed I had faith, but did I? Faith didn't keep me in that position; a lack of faith kept me in that position. I was afraid to look for, and start, something new.

We can sometimes feel like God isn't moving fast enough, and we get the urge to take things into our own hands. It brings to mind Sarai and Abram. God promised Abram a son, but God was not moving fast enough for Sarai, so she devised her own plan. Yes, God wanted a child for them, but not Sarai's way. Sarai wanted what she wanted and believed time was running out. Her lack of faith in God's ability to fulfill His promise led her to do something she should not have. She didn't take a moment to think that if God wants something for us, while there may be action required of us, that action will never require us to do something sinful. She needed faith to wait.

Other times we need to use our faith in God to act. Luke chapter eight tells of a woman who had suffered a horrible affliction for 12 years, and no doctor could help. With all her heart and mind, this woman believed that if she could do something even as simple as touch the fringe of the cloak of Jesus, He could heal her. She acted according to her faith, and Jesus told her it was her faith that made her well.

A CALL TO ACTION

Is there something in your life that you are rushing? Are you ill-equipped to handle it, or are your actions causing you to sin to complete it? Slow down. Pray for patience, wisdom, and self-control.

Or, is there something in your life where you are causing the Lord to wait on you? Has God blessed you with everything you need, including an open door, and you are simply refusing to walk through it? Pray for increased faith and strength to do whatever it is that you know you must.

SCRIPTURES

- ❖ Genesis 12:1-7
- ❖ Genesis 16:1-16
- ❖ Psalm 27:14
- ❖ Romans 8:25
- ❖ Mark 5:25-34
- ❖ James 2:14-20

PRAYER

Father, there are things in my life that I desire so intensely that I may fail to realize I need Your help. Please give me the wisdom to discern those times when I must wait on You and when I'm making You wait on me and, Father, in each of those times, please help me act as You would have me to.

12

CHASING REWARDS

"'I, the Lord, search the heart, I test the mind, even to give to each man according to his ways, according to the results of his deeds'" (Jer. 17:10).

Mom and Dad were old school. They never had to tell us their word was law; it was an unspoken agreement within our house. Even with this agreement, they still struggled with us when it came to keeping the house clean. We always invented ways to get out of doing housework and were clever about it too. There was a time when Dad bought a new cleanser for the bathtub for Leslie and me to use, but first, he wanted to demonstrate how to use it.

He sat on the edge of the tub, took out a rag and put a quarter-sized dollop of the cleanser on the rag, and said, "You only need about this much, then you scrub like this."

Leslie and I were standing behind him as he demonstrated how to clean the spot on the tub. Pointing to a different area, I asked, "Well, how much would you use on a spot like that?"

"The same amount." He said as he poured another quarter-sized dollop on the rag and cleaned the spot. Leslie caught on and then added, "I don't think that would be enough to clean that part over there."

"Yeah, it would. This stuff is pretty good. Watch." Then, he started to pour another dollop. Suddenly, he stopped pouring, then looked at us, and we all started laughing.

Usually, my parents stuck to the method of "Get your chores done or else." However, there was this one time when they tried something a little different.

On this occasion, they called us into the living room and told us they'd hidden money throughout the house. We could keep whatever money we found, but there was a catch; wherever we found the money, we had to clean the area before taking the cash from it. This was an unprecedented move by our parents. They rarely showed a creative side when attempting to get us to do something they wanted us to do. I was young but not stupid, and I had so many questions. If I didn't feel like doing anything, was this a voluntary experiment? Did the dirtier spots pay more? If I found one of the others didn't do a good job cleaning an area and I finished it, would they have to split the cash with me?

Unfortunately, their creativity didn't pay off, pun intended. I suppose our parents thought, incorporating the reward with the work would result in better motivation. That wasn't the case at all. We didn't care about the work. All we wanted was the reward. I don't believe we cleaned any of the areas the way our parents had intended for us to clean them. My parents learned two things that day. First, they realized they had five potential track stars living under that roof as they watched us race through the house. Second, they also learned there was no bribery in the world strong enough to motivate us to clean behind the toilet. I, personally, didn't care if there was a one-hundred-dollar bill back there and if Ralph, Ronnie, Bobby,

Ricky, and Mike were waiting to serenade me with *Candy Girl*, I still wasn't going to clean behind the toilet voluntarily.

In the end, when creativity lost out, Mom and Dad resorted back to their old school ways. It wasn't nearly as profitable for us, but it did get the job done.

In June of 2012, Leslie called me and told me she was joining a direct sales company called Thirty-One Gifts, and she wanted me to join her team. I was in shock because this was so not a Leslie kind of thing. Thirty-One Gifts sold items such as purses, wallets, and totes. I politely told my sister no but that I would buy from her to support her. I never gave my decision another thought. I ended up joining a week later after waking from a dream, where I was told to join. Deciding to join was a total leap of faith because I had sworn off such companies after two previously failed attempts to make money as a consultant with a different company. I told myself I'd be happy to make a couple extra hundred dollars a month, and I'd consider anything more than that, gravy, at least that was how I felt before I learned about the Leadership Incentive Trips.

LIT, as it was called, was a week-long, all expenses paid trip out of the country. John and I had never taken a proper vacation together, and I saw earning the trip as the way to remedy that. It was too late to earn the trip for 2013, but I worked hard and earned it for 2014. Traveling and experiencing the fun with other consultants on my team and spending time with my husband made me crave the next trip scheduled in 2015. However, as I worked to achieve the goal for 2015, I began to struggle. My sales were lacking, so I brainstormed for ways to get my numbers where I needed them to be.

I looked at what other consultants were doing and found that many of them would conduct donation drives. They would sell the bags or totes, and the customers would donate them back to the consultant. The consultant would then give them away as care bags to patients in a hospital or residents in a shelter. I thought the idea was brilliant! I was primarily interested in donating to children, so I started making calls to hospitals and treatment facilities to see if they would be interested in the donations. I had to leave a message with each hospital I called. Before any of the facilities could return my phone calls, I started to feel horrible. I knew the donations would be appreciated and that I wouldn't make any money, but I still knew this would help me earn the trip. I didn't feel right. It felt selfish, so I decided not to go forward.

The next day, one of my calls was returned. After the caller identified himself and from which facility he was calling, he proceeded to tell me they didn't treat children.

"Well, thank you for calling me back," I replied. "It's just as well. I've decided not to proceed with the donations."

"Oh," he said, somewhat disappointed. "I was actually calling to tell you we were interested in accepting what you have."

"The bags I planned on donating are for kids. If you don't treat children, how could you use them?"

"We don't treat children, but we see children here every day," he said. "They come with their parents. Sometimes they're with their parents when the family receives horrible news. Or, sometimes, they are sitting beside their mom or dad as they're receiving treatment." He explained that what many people don't realize is when a parent is fighting a life-threatening illness, the child is battling it too.

"It would be nice to be able to give them something like a coloring book or anything. When we can give the children something, it truly makes a difference."

The trip was still on my mind, but it took a backseat. It was no longer my *why*. I completely immersed myself in working on getting as many bags donated as possible. I started what some told me I should have turned into a non-profit. I didn't just sell the bags and donate them. I reached out to the community and asked if they wanted to help make the bags something special. I tried to make it something that anyone could be a part of, and it was my wish for each child who received a bag to feel that someone out there cared about them. I wanted the bags to look like gifts.

So, I recruited volunteers. Inside every bag was a plain brown 8" x 8" x 8" box that contained crayons, magazines, coloring books, bubbles, etc. The volunteers decorated the boxes. The volunteers were children at daycare centers, high school sports teams, and coworkers who decorated the boxes as a family activity. Then, more volunteers came together, and we formed assembly lines to help make sure each bag contained all it was supposed to include. We tagged each bag with a handwritten message that included the name of the donator. It was an incredible feeling for all who were involved. The boxes were the best part. Some were decorated with stick figures because a four-year-old decorated them, and some were skillfully decorated with Disney and Marvel characters. Everyone involved felt a sense of joy because we all had a common and utterly unselfish goal of putting a smile on a child's face. We did this a few times over the year, and all together, we donated more than 400 bags to three different hospitals! It was grand, and my heart was not focused on a trip, making it even better.

THE LESSON

As Christians, we should understand that God wants to bless us for our work, but we also must know that being rewarded should not be our motivator. We have jobs that entice us with bonuses, pay raises, and promotions, and we have earthly bosses who don't care about our attitudes as long as we complete our work. On the other hand, our Heavenly Father does care about our attitudes, perhaps even more so than the work. Remember, He is a searcher of hearts and minds.

Using material rewards as a motivator can be a hit or miss. In my parent's case, it was an abysmal disaster. We wanted the reward but no part of the work. Our hearts weren't in it. There was no pride associated with having a job well done. There was no desire to make sure Mom and Dad were happy with our cleaning, nor did we care to stand back and say, "Wow! We did a great job."

In contrast, when I decided to donate the bags to the hospital, the happiness of others became my primary focus. I was not concerned with what I would get. That shift in my mindset made it easier to absorb every rejection I heard while marketing my way to a sale. God wants us to feel purpose in our work and to give it our all. Why else would He instruct us to work as though working for Him in all that we do?

A CALL TO ACTION

Take pride in whatever you do and put your heart into it! Think of how you help others and then make serving your purpose. Whatever work you do, that work exists because it's necessary. Bring joy to what you do and work as though God, Himself, gave you that duty. Use the blank sheets in this chapter to make a list of the positive differences your work makes. No matter what you do, please know that you make a difference. Describe how your family is better off because of what you do. How are your customers better off? How is your employer better off? How are your employees better off? Make a list of how you can improve the differences you already make. Keep in mind that your work attitude will be noticed and make a difference in those around you.

SCRIPTURES

- ❖ Proverbs 16:3
- ❖ 1 Corinthians 10:31
- ❖ Colossians 3:23-24

PRAYER

Lord, thank You! You've given me an essential role in life. Because of the work, You've given me to do, the life of someone else is made better, including my own. Father, please guide my attitude and my heart, and may I never forget to thank You for blessings, always remembering the real blessing is in the work You've trusted me to do.

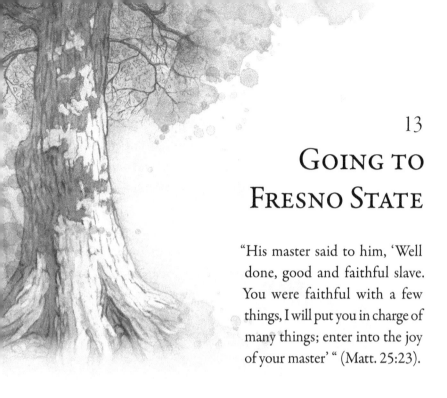

13

GOING TO FRESNO STATE

"His master said to him, 'Well done, good and faithful slave. You were faithful with a few things, I will put you in charge of many things; enter into the joy of your master' " (Matt. 25:23).

Shortly after I graduated high school, some of my friends who were attending Fresno State asked if I wanted to spend the weekend with them at the dorms. I already knew my parents weren't going to allow me to take the car to Fresno, which was an hour away from Atwater. Just asking to take the car was a significant hurdle alone, but to take it so I could stay in the dorms at a college. That was a huge ask.

I knew it would take some convincing. I wanted to go in the worst way. The whole A-Town Posse was going (yes, that's what we called ourselves, don't judge). I had to make sure not one, but both of my parents were in at least somewhat of a good mood when I asked. There was a strategy to asking Mom and Dad for something. I weighed my options and predicted the outcomes of the different tactics I could use.

I also had to factor in the others, meaning my siblings. I had to know if any of them had already asked Mom and Dad for something outlandish that day. Our parents only had the tolerance for one, maybe two, crazy requests like this, once every few days. Had any of them already worked what Mom referred to as 'her last nerve'? Asking for something this big was a process with a lot of moving parts.

I planned to ask Dad first, and I knew the best time to do that was as soon as he got home from work. I knew he would tell me to ask Mom, but I would be in a much better position if I could get the ok from him. That was always better than asking Mom cold. Unfortunately, I messed up my perfect opportunity due to an error in my judgment. I had the stereo playing too loudly when Dad came home on the day I planned to ask. Instead of coming into the house ready to relax, he came in livid.

He walked into the house and yelled, "Turn that music down! It's rocking the house!" I might have been able to recover and salvage the situation had it not been for Lucretia, who completely misjudged the moment's seriousness. She ran to Dad, jumped in front of him, and started to do 'The Wop,' while singing a song she made up on the spot,

"Rocking the house
rock, rock, rockin' the house"

Our father's expression was stone cold as he looked down at her from his 6'4" frame. If he had been Superman, red beams would have shot out of his eyes and reduced her to ash. When Lucretia finally realized that Dad was not amused, she didn't have the sense to stop immediately and walk away. No, instead, she let the song and the dance trail off, slowly and painfully.

"Rockin...the...house," she sang, with each word becoming a little quieter and each dance move becoming less animated.

"Rock... rock... roooockin..."

I wisely decided to ask the next day.

Because I lost a day, and the weekend was right around the corner, these circumstances forced me to go with Plan B. Plan B was to bite the bullet and ask Mom and Dad simultaneously. Plan B required preparation. I practiced what to say and how to say it. Once I felt prepared, I walked into their room, with my memorized approach and all of my counterarguments, ready to go. I took a deep breath, looked at my mother, and said, "Mom," then turned to my father and said, "Dad." Then I quickly said, "Can I take the car and spend the weekend in Fresno with Carmel and Cherise -"

"Sure," Mom interrupted.

"Cause studies show - Wait, what?"

"You can go," Mom said.

Like a fool, instead of taking that "W" and running for the keys, I asked, "Just like that?"

"Yeah, we trust you and your friends," Dad replied.

I am so thankful because that was just the first of many trips to Fresno, and thirty years later, Carmel, Cherise, Deon, Nicola, Shawn, Jack, Maurice, and the rest of the A-Town Posse still reminisce about those days!

I've often thought about the differences between our two children. It amazes me how polar opposite they are from each other. For example, I once got a phone call from Jacob's teacher, asking us to help her bring Jacob out of his shell. He was a sweet, quiet child, but his teacher felt he kept to himself a little too much. He had a small circle of friends (whom he still has today, many of whom were groomsmen in his wedding), but his teacher was concerned that he was a little too shy. It took some time, but Jacob did finally come out of his shell.

Jordan, on the other hand, was a diva from the crib and destined to be popular. When she was in kindergarten, I got a call from her elementary school about her hair. Under normal circumstances, I would put a lot of time into Jordan's hair before sending her to school, either braiding it or putting it into some cute design with ponytails. On the morning of the phone call from her school, I was in a hurry, so I gave her two basic ponytails. When I drove her to school, she didn't want to get out of the car. I didn't know why. What I did know was that I was going to be late for work, so I told her to hurry. She tried to grab one of her dad's baseball caps that was sitting in the backseat. I gave her a quizzical glance but didn't think much of the action. I told her to leave the hat, get out of the car, and get to class. Approximately 15 minutes later was when I received the phone call from the principal at Jordan's school.

"Hi, is this Jordan's mom?" she asked.

"Yes, this is Silvia. Everything ok?"

"Oh, everything is fine," she said. "We were wondering if it would be ok for the school nurse to change Jordan's hairstyle."

"Huh?"

"Jordan is here in the office. She told us she isn't going to class with her hair in its current state."

"Thank you for attempting to clean it up. I appreciate you," I said, "but I know Jordan, and I know those weren't her words. What did that child say?"

"Well, um, her actual words were," the principal replied somewhat hesitantly, " 'I ain't going to class with my head looking like this.' " She paused a moment. I was hoping she hadn't heard the slight laugh I accidentally allowed to escape. Then she continued,

"We tried to tell her that her hair is beautiful just the way it is, but she's pretty determined. Class has started, and she refuses to go."

I tried, but I could not be upset with Jordan because I knew how I would feel if I was in public and thought my hair looked busted. I had to admit she got this from her mama. So, I permitted the nurse to change her style.

Aside from the differences in their personalities, there is also a substantial difference in how my children handle money. When it comes to finances, Jake is a pace car, and Jordan is a race car. When Jacob was 23 years old, he proposed to his girlfriend, Alma. He was living with roommates at that time and knew he needed to save money. We made him an offer to move back home to allow him to save on rent, and he accepted. After a year and a half of saving, Jacob and Alma were able to pay cash for their wedding. Jacob also purchased a new car, and they were able to get the apartment they wanted and begin their life together in the way they wanted. In contrast, the only way Jordan will save money is to save for something that will happen within the next two months.

Much to Jordan's dismay, I told her if I were to come into a large sum of money, while I would give Jacob his share in full, I would give hers to her in allotments. She is my race car, whose drive and ambition serve her well in so many ways but not when it comes to money, and I know that.

THE LESSON

Lesson after lesson, we're told of the importance of trusting God, but how often do we consider we need to be trustworthy as well? Are we working to be trusted so that we can be trusted with more? During my high school years, I had no idea that I was building trust with my parents. I never sneaked out of the house, I never got drunk,

I never skipped school, and I didn't use foul language. I won't try to pretend I was an angel (my parents never did find out about me cheating in Spanish class, and Dad won't know until he reads about it in this book), but I handled enough responsibilities correctly to help them feel as though they could trust me with more. In dealing with my children, I couldn't help but remember I am still a child of God, and I began to wonder what blessings He might be holding back from me because I'm not demonstrating that I am responsible enough to have them?

Scripture says God will give us the desires of our heart, but He knows which of His children can handle such blessings and which of them need a metered approach. Often, when things in life seem to be going great, we neglect God. We find other things to do with our time, rather than devoting some of it to studying scripture, prayer, and building our relationship with our Lord. We put material things before our devotion to Him, and this is why it is easier for a camel to go through the eye of a needle than it is for a wealthy person to enter the Kingdom of God.

Sadly, sometimes our attention is only brought back to Him when things start to unravel. God's ultimate desire for us is salvation, and if He can't trust that blessings won't cause our relationship with Him to suffer, how can He lavish us with blessings? God must come first, in times of hardship, as well as times of comfort, and not because we are chasing rewards! Remember, God is a searcher of hearts. It's not until we put His will before our own that He is able to trust us with His blessings. Put Him first, and all things become possible, even a camel going through the eye of a needle. Think of Solomon. When Solomon was told to ask for whatever he wanted, he asked for wisdom to govern God's people and, because he put God first, God blessed Solomon with much more than he'd asked. A blessing isn't just a gift from God; it's a responsibility. Christians should desire salvation more than earthly blessings, so until we can be trusted not to let our relationship with God be impaired, it's in our best interest for God to give us only our daily bread.

A CALL TO ACTION

Strengthen God's trust in you by tirelessly working on your relationship with Him. Commit time daily to reading your Bible and to prayer. If time escapes you during the day, go to bed just a little earlier and wake up just a little earlier and devote the first moments of your day to your relationship with God.

SCRIPTURES

- ❖ 1 Kings 3:1-15
- ❖ 1 Kings 4:29-34
- ❖ Matthew 6:9-13
- ❖ Matthew 25:14-30
- ❖ Mark 10:17-27

PRAYER

Lord, thank You for loving me enough to bless me in ways You know will not cause me to stumble. I pray that every day will strengthen my love and devotion to You.

14

LUCRETIA AND THE LEAVES

"Therefore the law is ignored and justice is never upheld. For the wicked surround the righteous; Therefore justice comes out perverted" (Hab. 1:4)

When we were kids living in California, we had a huge tree in our yard, and every autumn, the leaves would fall and cover the ground. One Wednesday, Gina and Wesley raked the leaves into a large pile but didn't dispose of them. Instead, they left them in the yard. I think it's because they didn't have time to finish the job before we had to leave for Wednesday night Bible Study with our dad.

When we returned home from Bible study, there sat what seemed like a mountain of leaves. The sun had gone down, and we kids were content to leave the pile alone until the following day. But our dad was not. Instead of having the two youngest complete the job they started, he instructed the three oldest to do so. Leslie and I dutifully picked up the tools for the task and headed for the pile. Lucretia, however, stood in place, indignant to the command. Leslie and I thought she hadn't heard Dad, so we reiterated what our dad instructed us to do.

Lucretia very plainly and clearly said, "I'm not sticking my hands in that pile. We can't see and there could be 'dog-do' in there."

Les and I immediately turned to Dad, waiting for the hammer to fall, because we knew he heard Lucretia's blatant defiance as clearly as we had. To our surprise and horror, Dad did nothing. He didn't move a single muscle or say a single word! I looked at Leslie, and she looked at me, both of us completely confused and wondering what in the world was happening. How could our sister boldly declare she would not do as she was told and our father be ok with it? Leslie dropped the rake, I dropped the garbage bag, and we ran to our dad. Perhaps he was suffering from a stroke. That was the only explanation for his lack of action.

"Daddy, did you hear Lucretia?" we asked. "She's not helping! Make her help, like you told her."

Dad remained still and – worse – silent. Leslie picked up the rake, I returned to the garbage bag, and we both got to work. The entire time we were loading leaves into the bag, we spoke to each other in a tone silent enough for our father not to hear but loud enough for Lucretia to hear. It was a fine line, but we walked it with ease.

"I hate her. That's why she's gonna grow up to be ugly," I said.

"Grow up to be? She's already there." Leslie replied, and we both began to laugh.

Lucretia, of course, didn't find it funny. She decided to answer our comments in her Lucretia-like fashion. She strolled over to us, locked eyes with me, and, without breaking that eye contact, she slowly started to bend at the knees as though doing a squat. She reached down with her thumb and index finger, picked up one single leaf, and dropped it in the bag I was holding. For someone so concerned with dog-do, she sure didn't seem to care at that moment because even as she reached down to pick up a leaf, she never broke eye contact with me. Next, she fixed her gaze on Leslie and repeated the action in the same slow, deliberate manner. She accidentally picked up two leaves and made it a point to let the extra one fall back to the ground. Dad stood in the distance and watched it all.

Leslie and I looked at each other and, without the need to express it verbally, we both understood that from that point forward, our parents might consider Lucretia one of us, but we didn't! She'd been excommunicated! No more trading candy with her at Halloween. On her birthday, we weren't going to sing. When we visited our grandmother, if Lucretia was the one in trouble and Gramp asked Leslie or me to get a switch from the tree, we were going to get the biggest one we could find, preferably one with fruit still attached!

Once we'd disposed of all the leaves, we headed into the house to clean the kitchen. I was assigned wash duty, Leslie was drying, Lucretia was cleaning the countertops, and Dad was sitting at the table quietly watching. I couldn't take it anymore. I had to say something. I had to know why Lucretia hadn't suffered the wrath that should have come with disobedience.

I asked my dad, "Daddy, why didn't you do anything? Leslie and I picked up all the leaves, and Cretia only picked up two!"

Dad remained silent, refusing to answer my question. Lucretia, however, had become cocky with her newly found amnesty, and, as she walked past our dad, she looked back at me and touted, "I didn't pick up two leaves. I picked up three."

That's when it happened! The moment for which Leslie and I had been waiting. Dad finally snapped into action. As Lucretia attempted to stroll past him, still very proud of her "I picked up three." comment, Dad jumped in front of her, and before our eyes had a chance to tell our brains what we'd just seen, we heard the *gluck* sound. Dad had popped Lucretia right on her lips with the palm of his hand while her mouth was still open. The sound it made was not only hilarious, but it was also the sound of sweet justice! The total and complete look of shock on Lucretia's face, coupled with the sound made by palm-to-lips contact, was more than Leslie and I could take. Our stomachs hurt as we fought to hold in the laughter. We knew we weren't supposed to laugh at each other when one of us got punished, so we tried to hide our faces from our dad. I opened the fridge's top freezer door and stuck my head in to try to hide my face. Leslie was trying to hide her face behind a large salad bowl while acting like she was drying it. Lucretia knew we were laughing at her from the depths of our souls. The humiliation of being brought down a few notches is what made her cry, and the sight of her tears forced audible laughter out of Leslie and me.

Our father allowed us both to laugh and sent Lucretia to bed, letting her out of kitchen duty. We didn't care.

Years later, while with my family, we were recounting that night's events and laughing about it, I asked my dad again why he waited to punish her. His answer was simple enough. He said, "I wasn't going to be told by my children when I was going to act on something or how I was going to act on something."

THE LESSON

We never want to feel as though God is sitting by, watching evil or wrongdoing occur and doing nothing about it. In this world, we see examples of those who do not fear God seemingly getting away with sinful acts. God is not asleep. He has not forgotten His laws and commands. It is not up to us to decide how and when God should act. Those who aren't obeying God should not mistake His patience for a free pass. God knows the lessons He's teaching and to whom He's directing those lessons. The decision of when to discipline, punish, and show mercy belongs to God and God alone.

A CALL TO ACTION

Have you ever thought you needed to hold God to His word? Have you ever felt as though He was asleep at the wheel while you were in the passenger's seat of life, yelling for Him to wake up? Do you get angry or question Him when He doesn't act the way you believe He should? Give total control over to Him. God has not lost sight of the best way to handle troubles in your life. There is a lesson even in his stillness. Trust Him.

SCRIPTURES

- ❖ Psalm 31:14-15
- ❖ Proverbs 3:5
- ❖ Proverbs 15:3
- ❖ Habakkuk 1:2-4
- ❖ Romans 9:14-16

PRAYER

Father, please help me to be still when You are still. I will trust You always in all ways.

15

Sweet Potato Pie

> "But He said, 'On the contrary,
> blessed are those who hear the
> word of God and observe it.' "
> (Luke 11:28)

My siblings and I had rules. Here are some of the rules, as I remember them, as given to us by our parents:

1. When we get into the store, don't ask for anything.
2. Don't slam that door!
3. When visiting our friends, don't act like you're hungry.
4. Be back inside when the streetlights come on.
5. Don't talk back (rolling of the eyes was considered a silent version of breaking this rule).
6. Don't put family business in the street, i.e., what happens in this house stays in this house.
7. Don't act like you're grown.
8. We ain't one of your little friends.
9. Eat what's cooked or don't eat.
10. Don't play outside in your school clothes.

11. If one of you gets into a fight, you all get into that fight.

There was no order for these rules, and one was no more important than the others. Rule #5 was slightly different, though, because it didn't only apply to my parents. It extended to aunts, uncles, teachers, and babysitters. When I was in the fourth grade, I acted as though I forgot about Rule #5, and I raised my voice and talked back to our babysitter, Ms. Laura Mae. Ms. Laura Mae was around the same age as my grandmothers and, like my grandmothers, she did not tolerate disrespect from children. She would come to our home and watch us in the morning after Mom and Dad left for work. She would stay with Gina and Wesley throughout the day and make sure Lucretia, Leslie, and I caught the bus and made it to school.

I don't remember the circumstances which led to my temporary insanity on this fateful morning, but I do remember the look on Ms. Laura Mae's face when I yelled back at her. Her neck straightened and her head pulled back a little, her eyebrows raised, and her eyes widened. I immediately knew I had messed up. Not only had I broken Rule #5, but that look on her face also said I had broken Rule #7! Then she said the words that were going to haunt me for the next nine hours. She said, "I'm telling your daddy."

I knew I was going to be in big trouble when my dad got home that day. Despite my impending doom, I tried my best to enjoy my school day. It was a failed attempt. With my mother, the punishment was swift, but it would last for what felt like hours with Dad. A part of dad's punishment always included a lecture. The kind of lecture that would make a kid ask for extra chores if it meant not having to listen to another word. I knew I would hear how talking back to an adult in his day meant the taste was going to be slapped out of his mouth, or that he was going to be knocked into next week, or the black was going to get slapped off him.

Also, with Dad, you never knew when it was going to end. He would leave, and just when you thought it was over, he would come back and say, "And another thing!" Then, when it really was over, and you were sitting there crying and wishing he'd get struck by lightning, he would come back once more and say something silly like, "Punishing you hurts me more than you." Then, he'd ask for a hug. In retrospect, dreading the punishment proved to be a lot worse than the punishment itself.

Before my mother passed away, I had gotten into the habit of calling her every Thanksgiving. Of course, I would wish her a happy Thanksgiving, but the call's main point was to get her to walk me through making a sweet potato pie. I grew up making sweet potato pies alongside my mother and, if not for that fact, there would be no way I would have been able to follow her recipe, as she instructed during those phone calls. I never called because I needed the recipe. I called because I loved hearing her tell me the recipe. Each year I would follow along while she told me what to do.

"Do you have the yams?" she would ask.

"Yes, ma'am," I'd reply.

"Ok, heat them up. You know how many yams you need, right?"

"Yes, ma'am."

"Ok, put the yams in a bowl after they're heated, then put some butter in with them and mix it up really good."

"Ok, done!"

"Alright, put an egg in there too."

"It's in there."

"Next, put some flour in it until it's the right consistency." It's at this point I would usually start to giggle as I continued to follow her instructions. "If you put too much flour in there, put in a little milk. If you use too much milk, put a little more flour in it."

"Ok, mom. It's looking good," I would say.

"Ok, put sugar in until it tastes like it's supposed to." At this point in the conversation, my giggles would usually turn into full-blown laughter. She continued, "Ok, next, and this is important, get the nutmeg! Go crazy with the nutmeg. The nutmeg is what's gonna make the difference. Nutmeg is what makes the pie!"

"Alright, mom. Nutmeg has been added."

"Mix it all up and pour it into the pie crusts and put the pies in the oven at 350 degrees until they're done."

Once the pies were in the oven, she would tell me to call her later to let her know how they turned out. They always turned out perfectly.

THE LESSON

We can, and should, think of the Word of God as a manual for how to live life. It's our perfect guide, or recipe, for salvation. Although it is impossible to earn salvation, we are still called to live our lives in a Godly way. Just as children can recite a list of rules they must follow; Christians also have a list of rules (commands) we must follow. There are those times when we will fall short and yell at the babysitter, and discipline may follow, but if we repent, our Heavenly Father always forgives. We don't get to decide which of His commands we will or will not obey. They are all there for our submission, and all are important. We don't have the liberty to point at one scripture and say, this scripture says this is what I must do to be saved and then ignore other scriptures that also point to necessary actions for salvation. His Word tells us the way to salvation, and it takes that recipe in its entirety to produce that perfect result.

Take the topic of baptism, for example. We will adhere to Romans 10:9

"that if you confess with your mouth Jesus as Lord, and believe in your heart that God raised Him from the dead, you will be saved;"

but will ignore scriptures such as John 3:5

"Jesus answered, 'Truly, truly, I say to you, unless one is born of water and the Spirit he cannot enter into the kingdom of God.' "

I equate this to the importance my mother stressed on nutmeg in her pie. I never picked the recipe apart, nor when I was a child did I assign my own level of importance to the rules my parents had given us, deciding which I would obey and willingly ignore. Not once would I have heard the words, *nutmeg is what makes the pie,* and then concluded, sugar was not necessary. Although she chose that moment in our conversation to stress the importance of the nutmeg, it didn't invalidate the necessity of the other ingredients.

We should not assign our own level of importance to what Christ has instructed in the New Testament. If the Lord commanded it, He did so for a reason. Imagine if Simon said it didn't matter if he put the net on the right side or the left because they'd been out all night, and the fish weren't biting. Total obedience matters to God.

A CALL TO ACTION

Are you willingly ignoring a command of God? Have you assigned one of His commands as a low priority in your life and, therefore, as something that isn't worth following? Are you applying your own logic to why a command exists? Remember, all of God's commands are about making you better and your salvation. If there is a commandment you know you are ignoring, study and make a list of the reasons you can find in scripture that explains why that command exists. Learn about how obeying that command will please the Lord and make your life better. Allow that list to empower you as you commit to obedience.

SCRIPTURES

- ❖ 1 Samuel 15:22-23
- ❖ Matthew 7:24-27
- ❖ John 21:2-7
- ❖ James 1:22-25

PRAYER

Father, I am aware there are forces at work attempting to keep me apart from You. I'm disheartened to admit that some of those forces are from within. I acknowledge that there are times I knowingly disobey Your commands to satisfy a desire of the flesh, or I submit to tradition or peer pressure instead of remaining steadfast in that which You would have me to do. Lord, may I never assign my own value system to Your commands.

16

Take Care of You, for Me

"And He said to him, 'You
shall love the Lord your
God with all your heart,
and with all your soul,
and with all your mind'"
(Matt. 22:37).

W hen I was younger, my parents would tell us to do something, and then they would trust that we would do it. More times than I care to admit, that ended up being a mistake for them and us. When we were kids, we would do what we were told because we were scared to death of the consequences if we didn't. However, there were times when the things we wanted to do outweighed or distracted us from the things we were told to do, like the day our mother told us to keep an eye on the chicken.

I was around 14 years old, which means Leslie and Lucretia would have been approximately 12 and 11. The chicken was on the stove boiling, and Mom gave us orders to make sure it didn't burn while she and Dad ran a few errands.

"Yes, ma'am." We dutifully replied.

As soon as Mom and Dad left the house, I went back to my room to continue watching television. I don't know what Leslie and Lucretia were doing, but one thing I do know is they weren't watching the chicken either. I don't remember how much time passed before Leslie asked, "Y'all smell something?"

No one answered the question out loud. We all knew that was the smell of burnt chicken and whoopins. We were in big trouble. We didn't know when to expect our parents back, but we weren't going to accept our fate without a fight, so we came up with a plan! The first order of business was to get rid of the smell. That was Lucretia's job. Second, we had to clean the pot in which the chicken had been cooking. That was my job. Third, we had to scrape, carefully, the burnt pieces off the chicken. That was Leslie's job. Once we all knew our assignments, we got to work!

We had no idea how much time we had to execute the plan, so we moved quickly. Lucretia grabbed the ammonia we used when mopping. Usually, we would dilute it with water, but this time there was no diluting. We needed the ammonia at full strength! She doused a rag with the ammonia then ran up and down the hallway dragging the rag along the walls. She had to open all the windows to prevent us from dying from the fumes.

Leslie and I were in the kitchen. We carefully dumped the chicken into a colander over the sink while letting the burnt, nasty water go down the drain. Leslie then took the colander over to the garbage can, where she began to peel away any traces of burnt chicken. The trick was to remove all burnt areas but still look like it hadn't been peeled. She also had to leave enough of the good parts to eat. We knew Leslie had the steadiest hands. She always won when we played *Operation*, so she was the logical choice for this part of the plan. Leslie had to move quickly but not too quickly. I didn't envy her. The pressure was great.

While Leslie tended the chicken with the skill of an 11-year-old surgeon, and Lucretia ran up and down the hallway like a track star,

I started my job of cleaning the pot. This pot was not one of those Teflon, non-stick, cookware kind of pots. It was a large stainless-steel stockpot, and cleaning it took elbow grease, three *Brillo* pads, and a dull knife. My weak little arms were on fire as I scrubbed and scraped, with all my might, as quickly as I could.

When Lucretia completed her task, she asked what else she could do. I told her to get the mop and bucket out, so if Mom and Dad questioned why the house smelled like ammonia, we could say to them we'd mopped the house while they were gone. In hindsight, I suppose we really could have mopped the house, but at the time, Lucretia running up and down the hallway with an ammonia-soaked rag just made more sense.

Once we'd removed all evidence of being burned from the chicken and the pot, we put the chicken back into the pot, covered it with water, and put it back on the stove! We walked away, giving each other high fives on a job well done, and went back to what we were doing earlier.

Yes, we burned the chicken again.

When Jordan was in the fourth grade, she began complaining about pain in her legs. We took her to several different doctors in various fields. Each doctor found nothing alarming wrong and attributed the problem to growing pains. When Jordan turned 14 years old, the pain worsened and began to spread to her arms as well. It was debilitating at times. It wasn't until the day after her 18th birthday when the doctors finally gave us a diagnosis. We learned Jordan had small fiber neuropathy. We thought giving a name to the pain would be the beginning of making it go away. We thought if we knew what we were fighting, we could develop a clear course of action. Unfortunately, that wasn't the case. They told us there was no cure. I wouldn't and still do not accept that. I learned that small fiber neuropathy could be a symptom of something else, and I decided if I could figure out what that something else was, I could help my daughter make this pain go away.

I bought Jordan any and everything that I heard could help. I bought magnesium, vitamin D, vitamin B, Deep Blue Rub, lidocaine, essential oils, and we bought her a very advanced tens unit. I advised her to take Epsom salt baths and even practice hypnosis. I asked her to pay attention to her diet, and I told her to stay hydrated and consider going gluten-free. You name it, and I asked her to try it.

After she graduated from high school, she moved out to start her life as a college student. During a visit to her apartment, she asked me to get something for her from her room. In her room, in plain sight, I saw a bag filled with remedies I had given her to try. Many of them remained unopened. My heart sank. Although I had told her to try these things, she had not done so. I didn't blame her. I had been grasping at straws, and I knew that. But with each new thing I asked her to try, I had hope that it would be the thing to make the pain go away forever.

I finally realized she must be the one to believe in the remedy. I no longer go out on my own attempting to find a solution, but I do regularly implore her to be mindful of her health. Many times, when I am on the phone with her, the last thing I will say to her before we hang up is, "Take care of you, for me." Sometimes, she does try things I ask, not because she's afraid of consequences, but because she loves me.

THE LESSON

The greatest commandment, found in Matthew 22:37, is that we love God with all our heart, soul, and mind. This commandment made sense to me, but I was often confused when I read John 14:15, *If you love Me, you will keep My commandments.*

How did obeying equal love? When I was a child, I obeyed my parents, but it surely wasn't because I loved them. As a child, I obeyed for fear of consequences. It was fear of consequences that led three young kids to devise *Operation Chicken Fix*, but fear isn't enough. Fear can't cultivate a lasting devotion nor a meaningful relationship.

I remained confused about what Jesus meant for years until I thought of the words I was saying to Jordan, "Take care of you, for me." Then I realized, all God's commands are for our betterment and salvation, every single one! We are to be joyful, grateful, forgiving. We're told not to worry and be slow to anger. Do you see a pattern?

It wasn't until I looked at the words of Christ through the eyes of a parent that I understood what He meant. I thought, *I love my daughter so much that I have told her the best thing she can do to show me she loves me is to take care of herself.* My happiness is directly connected to the happiness and well-being of my children.

God wants all of us, without exception, to be saved. His commandments aren't the same as me grasping at straws for a cure. His commandments are the cure! God loves us, and He wants us to love Him, and the way we show Him that love is by taking care of ourselves, by making sure Christ's sacrifice for our souls was not in vain. And how do we do that? We do that by obeying His commands. The best way to take care of ourselves is to obey His commands.

A CALL TO ACTION

Are you worried about something even though He's instructed you to cast your cares at His feet? Are you indulging in pleasures that may be harming you when you have been told your body is a temple? Do you see life as full of despair because you aren't counting it all joy? What might you be doing that isn't in your best interest?

Each day you are to follow His commandments, all of which are about making you better. Do something today to take care of you, for Him.

SCRIPTURES

- ❖ Deuteronomy 10:12-13
- ❖ Matthew 22:36-38
- ❖ John 14:15
- ❖ John 14:21
- ❖ 1 John 5:3

PRAYER

Father, Your love and faithfulness are great. Thank You for loving me and for providing me with instructions on how to show my love for You and how to take care of myself.

17

Steel Thumbs

"'You shall love your
neighbor as yourself'"
(Matt. 22:39).

There are absolutes in life, and there were absolutes in my family. For example, do not, under any circumstances, ask Gina for her opinion on an outfit unless you are absolutely ready for brutal honesty, good or bad. If you are to ride somewhere with Wesley, don't think you will make him late because, if you aren't ready on time, he will absolutely leave without you. When getting scolded by Dad, do not think he's done when he walks away because he is absolutely going to come back for another round and will kick off the second half of the lecture by saying, "And another thing..."

Another absolute was that if you so much as walked past Mom and touched her back, she was absolutely going to require you to spend the next few moments of your life giving her a massage. If she was sitting somewhere, with her feet up and one of us brushed her foot, a foot massage was now going to be in order. More than once, I can recall all of us watching a movie, and someone would move wrong and touch Mom's foot. She'd say, "Oh, massage that foot real quick."

There was no *real quick* when it came to giving Mom a massage! Once a massage began, there was no end. That's what made giving her a massage something from which we ran. You could easily be on massage duty through an episode of *Who's the Boss, Perfect Strangers, and Moonlighting* if you didn't start to complain of hand cramps.

It took a bit of time for us to realize that if one of us were put on massage duty, she would go down the list, and we'd all have to do it. So, we evolved. When one of us was absent-minded enough to graze Mom's foot or touch her back and get sucked into massage duty, the other four of us learned to scatter! It didn't matter what we were doing or how much fun we were having if we heard the words, "Baby, massage right there" we were all looking for an exit! A couple of us would claim we had to finish homework, while another would say they had to go to the bathroom, and another would claim they were going to finish cleaning the kitchen. As the four of us who were free would leave, we would make eye contact with the trapped one, then point and laugh at them, knowing we wouldn't see them again for, at the very least, a half-hour.

The truth is Mom deserved those massages. During that time, she worked as a cashier at the commissary, and she stood on her feet all day long. Clocking out of her job didn't mean her work was even close to being done. After work, she would come home and take care of five kids. When our dad deployed to Okinawa, Japan, for a year-long unaccompanied tour, it was Mom who took care of us. We were all under the age of ten. She was amazing. If anyone deserved a massage, it was her. As children, none of us could see that. Thankfully, our dad could. It was he who always finished off the massages. He also knew that if one of us started Mom down the massage path, he would be required to pick up where the last child left off. He didn't complain or claim he had homework.

My husband, John, is in sales. He spends eighty percent of his day driving around from one appointment to another. Sitting in a car and the stress of being in traffic has done his back a lot more harm than good. His back is like one big knot. I don't know why I never offered to give him a massage before, but one day he asked so, I went to work. After a couple of massages, he started referring to my thumbs as thumbs of steel. I have something of a gift for finding knots and applying pressure to loosen them, which really makes a noticeable difference in how he feels. Never do I run for cover when he asks me to massage his back. I want to do it for him. I try to make each massage better than the last. Whenever I give John a massage, I can't help but think about those times my mother would ask for one, and we would run.

Before Mom passed away, we were fortunate enough for my parents to make the trip from Florida to Arizona a few times to visit us. During one of those visits, while my mother was sitting at the dining table, Jacob walked behind her and brushed against the back of her shoulders, and I heard those words, "Baby, baby, massage right there." As she pointed to her left shoulder blade, Jacob had no idea what he'd just done. He had no clue he was never going to hear his grandma say, "Ok, that's good enough. You can stop." I took out my phone and snapped a picture of the moment because it really took me back. Instead of running as I had done as a child, I waited for my turn.

THE LESSON

The second greatest commandment is to love your neighbor as yourself. I realize my husband and my mother are higher in the pecking order than, say, a neighbor would be in my life, but the lesson here remains the same. Our hearts are to be in the right place as we serve one another. As we grow and seek Christ and His desire for us, we are to take on a servant's attitude, just as He did. We should look to help others, not because we are afraid of the consequences if we don't, nor because we will benefit somehow. We should serve each other – relatives, friends, neighbors, and even strangers – and do so with a willing heart. Helping others has its own rewards.

A CALL TO ACTION

Get thirty-one index cards. Write one action of servitude that you could do in a day (i.e., uplift someone, call a friend, donate, send a card, babysit to give a parent a break, etc.) on each card. If you aren't able to think of thirty-one different ways to serve in one sitting, that's ok. There is nothing to say that you can't have the same action written on more than one card! After you have your cards written, draw a card each day and carry out the activity written on the card. The following month shuffle your cards and begin again.

SCRIPTURES

- ❖ Matthew 5:16
- ❖ Matthew 22:36-39
- ❖ Matthew 25:34-40
- ❖ John 13:14-17

❖ Philippians 2:3-11
❖ Hebrews 6:10

PRAYER

Lord, thank You for blessing me! Thank You for providing me with talents and abilities that will allow me to serve those around me, just as Christ served those around Him. Help me to think of ways I can give back. May my actions come from a place of love, and may they shine a positive light on You.

18

PLAYING THE PIANO

"And every day, in the temple and from house to house, they kept right on teaching and preaching Jesus as the Christ" (Acts 5:42).

In the late '70s, when my age was still in the single digits, I remember my mother making the admirable decision to get into shape. Our dad was stationed overseas, and I think my mother wanted to make sure when he returned, she was in better shape than she was when he left. She was determined and had a goal! And she knew exercise was vital!

When my mother exercised, it was an event that involved her kids as well. A mom setting an example and getting her daughters involved sounds fantastic, doesn't it? I can still remember those workouts with my mom.

We kids did not do the entire workout with Mom. We saved our strength for when it was time to work abs. Abs always came at the end of the training, when Mom was pretty tired, but abs were a must. It was *literally* crunch time. Mom wanted that flat stomach, which all ads promised you'd get by doing ab exercises (of course, now we know you can't spot-reduce fat, but that's another topic for another day). Mom was tired, but the determination to get abs done was there. It was at this point, Leslie and I would join in. Mom would lay on the floor on her back, and I'd take her left hand while my sister would take her right. Then Mom would say, in a loud drill sergeant-type voice, "Pull!"

Together, we'd pull her up until she was in a crunch position, then we'd let her back down and hear her say, "One." Then, again she would say, "Pull! Two. Pull! Three." To ten, we would go. I know my sister and I got more from the ab workout than Mom ever did.

Thanks to COVID-19, being stuck in the house is a thing. So, to keep me from feeling like 2020 wouldn't amount to much, I made two big goals.

#1 – Write a book
#2 – Start playing the piano

To help me achieve Goal #2, in June, my husband bought me a keyboard and a one-year subscription to an online piano teaching service. Since you've read the chapter "My Favorite Time of Year," what I'm about to say will come as no surprise. I wanted to be able to play Christmas carols on the piano.

When my keyboard arrived, I set it up and immediately downloaded the app, and created my login. There was just one problem. I quickly realized I wanted to play, not learn. I skipped drills, fast-forwarded instructional videos, and paid no attention to music theory. I visualized at least being able to play one Christmas song smoothly by

December. In my head, my piano playing skills sounded awesome. In reality, it sounded like this, *ting, ting, ting, ting, ting, tiiiiinnnngggg.*

It didn't take long for me to admit that lots of practice and work would be in order if I were going to play even one song the way I wanted. I started doing the drills and watching the videos, but in the meantime, *ting, ting, tiiiinnnnngggg.*

THE LESSON

At some point in our lives, we've all wanted to reap the benefits of something we didn't truly work to attain. Mom wanted to do the work but felt as though she couldn't. She was tired, worn out, and exhausted. Mom saw the value in the work and wanted to reap the rewards, but without effort, it was impossible. When it came to learning the piano, I wanted to skip the work I disliked entirely. My mother, nor I, got the results we wanted.

Have you ever said, "God, I want to do Your will; use me in Your plan however You desire." Then, instead of taking any action, you sat back and waited for opportunities to serve the Lord to fall into your lap. You didn't actively seek the opportunities because, after all, you gave everything over to God, and now you were waiting for him to do the crunch for you.

Think about the apostles. The intensity with which they served the Lord is evident! They were zealous, willing participants in their service! Their devotion was not lackluster, and they didn't wait for opportunities to find them.

Nothing worth having comes from others pulling us through the motions or by skipping lessons and trying to take the easy road. The best rewards come when we combine passion and purposeful intent with our actions.

A CALL TO ACTION

Put your heart, mind, conviction, and determination into everything you do for God. If you are tired, remember your strength comes from God, and He will always supply you with what you need to do His will. Don't just be a *willing* participant but an *active* one; look for ways to serve Him. When you are actively searching, that's when opportunities will present themselves.

SCRIPTURES

- ❖ Proverbs 16:3
- ❖ 1 Corinthians 15:58
- ❖ Ephesians 2:8-10

PRAYER

Lord, I humbly give my life over to You. I pray You will present me with opportunities to do work that will further Your plan. I thank You for trusting me and for giving me the strength to complete the tasks. I know it is by grace I am saved and not by works, but I know there is work for me to do, and I respectfully and fearfully ask for Your guidance.

19

SHRUGGING SHOULDERS

"Do not grieve the Holy Spirit
of God, by whom you were
sealed for the day of redemp-
tion" (Eph. 4:30).

Everyone has that movie, that book, or that song, the one that no matter how many times you've seen it, read it, or heard it, it makes tears well up, just as it did the first time you came across it. For my mother, that movie was *Imitation of Life*, the 1959 adaptation. If you haven't seen it, I'm going to go out on a limb and say it probably isn't on your watchlist, so chances are you'll forgive me for giving away the ending.

The film follows two single mothers, Lorna and Annie. Lorna, white, hires Annie, black, as a caretaker for her daughter, Susie. Annie's daughter, Sara Jane, is technically African American, but her skin is extremely fair, allowing her to pass for white, which she fully embraces, because of the opportunities it affords her.

Annie loves Sara Jane deeply and only ever wants her daughter's love in return, while Sara Jane only longs for the privileges passing herself off as white provides. Throughout the movie, Sara Jane denies her true heritage up to, and including, denying her mother. When Sara Jane becomes an adult, she moves to a different city to get away from Annie and anyone who may know her true heritage. Annie travels to make one more visit to see her daughter just to hold her like she did when she was little. Instead of being overjoyed to see her mother, Sara Jane becomes outraged and vows to keep moving until her mother becomes too tired to continue looking for her. Annie puts her hurt feelings aside and promises never to bother Sara Jane again.

Now get ready for the tears. Annie dies. Lorna makes sure Annie has the funeral she wished for; lavish, in a large church, with a gospel choir and a horse-drawn hearse. The number of people in attendance at the funeral is a testimony to the kind of woman Annie was. Sara Jane makes it back to town in time to fight through the crowd and reach the hearse carrying her mother's casket. She throws open the doors on the back of the hearse and begins to sob over her mother's coffin. Through tears, she cries, "Mama, can you hear me? I'm so sorry, Mama. I did love you."

Whoa! That scene always gets me in the feels. As a kid, watching it with my mother, I never once saw her make it through that scene without crying. Please understand, my mother's tears weren't for Sara Jane. Her tears were for Annie because Annie was never going to be able to hear the words her daughter proclaimed that day, the words she longed to hear. I would totally understand if you wanted to put this book down so you could place a call to your mother really quick, just because.

Rejection can be blatant, like with Sara Jane and Annie, or it can be subtle, like with my dad and me on a long car ride. Before I go too much further, let me explain how much I hate long car rides. No, scratch that; I detest long car rides. Unless I am driving, the probability of me getting carsick is high. I can't read, look at my phone, or do much of anything to pass the time. I can't even turn to talk with backseat passengers. And, sometimes, no matter what I do, I can't stop that feeling of nausea from creeping up on me.

For this trip, I took the first driving shift, and after five hours, I relinquished the wheel to my friend. I was determined to enjoy this ride. I had my motion sickness bands, I focused on the horizon, and I had the air conditioning blowing in my face at full blast.

I was in the front passenger seat, and my father was in the backseat, directly behind me, sharing some hilarious anecdote about something that happened somewhere at some time. I mean, I have no idea what he and my friend were laughing about because I was way too preoccupied with trying not to throw up. While my father was telling his part of the story, every so often, he would reach out from the backseat, tap me on the shoulder and say, "You remember that, don't you, baby?" He followed his question with more laughter.

The laughing and the tapping continued.

"Remember when your mama said that?" tap, tap, tap.

"You couldn't have been more than five years old." tap, tap, tap.

"You were in kindergarten, and we told you when you got married, we were going to live with you and still tell you what to do." Tap, tap- I couldn't take it anymore. In frustration, and without a word, I shrugged away from the last tap.

His cheerful mood changed. He became quiet. Then I heard him ask, in a voice I'd never heard him use with me before, "Why did you do that? You kinda' hurt my feelings, baby." The tone of his voice hit me. My father had never before told me an action of mine hurt his feelings. He wasn't angry, and he didn't attempt to correct me. He was just hurt – hurt that his daughter could shrug him off, as I had just done.

I didn't care about the carsickness anymore. I'd just hurt my daddy! For some ridiculous reason, I didn't think that was even possible. Yes, I know he's human, but he was Dad. He was the man who was one half of the parental team who could strike fear in my heart, with just a glance, right up into my late teenage years. I couldn't possibly hurt his feelings, could I? An act, as simple as a disrespectful shrug of my shoulders, meant something to my dad because I meant something to my dad.

I think of that car ride every time I read 1 Samuel 8:7,

"The Lord said to Samuel, 'Listen to the voice of the people in regard to all that they say to you, for they have not rejected you, but they have rejected Me from being king over them.'"

THE LESSON

God has emotions. He feels love, hate, jealousy, and joy. He feels sorrow, He laughs, and His heart feels compassion. Have you ever pondered the thought that it could be possible for us to make God feel sorrow by shrugging Him off or by rejecting Him? Have you ever thought that choosing to spend free time watching television instead of dedicating some of that time to prayer could be the same as a shrug of your shoulder? How must God feel when we choose a hundred other things over Him? How often do we stop to think that only dedicating time to Him when we are hurt or in need might elicit emotions of sadness from our Father or possibly, even anger? God deeply desires a relationship with us, and we should desire one with Him.

A CALL TO ACTION

Starting today, make it a habit to say, "I love You, Lord" at least once a day. Allow that love for Him to influence your thoughts and actions.

SCRIPTURES

GOD feels love:

- ❖ Jeremiah 31:3
- ❖ John 3:16
- ❖ 1 John 4:8

GOD feels hate:

- ❖ Psalm 5:5
- ❖ Psalm 11:5
- ❖ Proverbs 6:16-19

GOD feels jealousy:

- ❖ Exodus 20:4-5
- ❖ Joshua 24:19-20

GOD feels joy:

- ❖ Isaiah 62:5
- ❖ Jeremiah 32:41
- ❖ Zephaniah 3:17

GOD feels grief and anger:

- ❖ Genesis 6:6
- ❖ Psalm 78:40-53

GOD feels compassion:

- ❖ Deuteronomy 32:36
- ❖ Judges 2:18
- ❖ Psalm 135:14

PRAYER

Father, thank You. Thank you for being my perfect example, and thank You for creating me in Your image. Because You made me as You have, I can understand a multitude of emotions and experiences, the paramount of them all being love. It is no mystery why the greatest commandment is to love You with all my heart, all my soul, and all my mind. Help me be ever mindful that my actions and behaviors cause You to feel happiness, anger, jealousy, and sorrow.

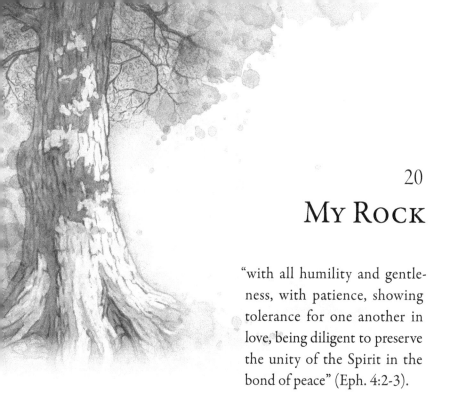

20

MY ROCK

"with all humility and gentleness, with patience, showing tolerance for one another in love, being diligent to preserve the unity of the Spirit in the bond of peace" (Eph. 4:2-3).

I came into the world blessed because of my mother and my father. They were the support and foundation of our family. No matter the circumstances, my siblings and I knew they were there for us, that they loved us and would stand up for us whenever we needed them to do so. They also stressed to us the importance of being there for each other. Within the walls of our home, we would argue and fight amongst ourselves from time to time, but there was no doubt of how much we cared for each other.

The family that my parents created was big, loud, and fun. We joked with each other, fought with each other, teased each other, and confided in each other. What I found most impressive about our family was my mom and dad's love for each other. After almost 50 years of marriage, my mother would still watch television snuggled up next to my dad. Until the day she passed away, it was common to hear her refer to my dad as *good-looking* or *fine*. And, to my father, the only one who came before my mother was God. When her health began to deteriorate, he was there for her every single day. And, still, he calls her *his baby*. My parent's union served as a solid foundation for us, but even more so, they were each other's foundation.

My parents set the bar for the family that I hoped to someday create for myself. I knew for me to have true happiness in a relationship, I had to have what they had. Love is a tremendous component, of course, but there must be more if the goal is to have a relationship with a solid, unshakeable foundation. There must be faith, trust, understanding, communication, and, most importantly, endurance. You don't reach 50 years together without endurance!

When you're young, and in love, it's possible to be blinded to what a real relationship requires. You might say the wedding vows, committing to stay in sickness and health, for richer or poorer, but at the first sign of struggle, couples can begin to wonder what they were thinking; marriage was not the happily ever after they thought it would be. That is because most of us enter marriage thinking about what we can get from it. We're going to have a family, we're going to have some babies, we're going to grow old together, and we're going to have a good life. Marriage is a commitment, a covenant. It requires us to think about what we can give as much as what we can receive.

The best marriages are formed by two people, giving all that they can to each other. Open and honest communication is often the first area where marriages begin to get cracks in their foundations.

When both spouses give everything they can to the marriage, they are more likely to be observant and aware of their spouse's needs.

I am blessed to have this kind of foundation with John. We recognize when the other is upset, even when the other is unwilling to admit to it. We seek to remedy issues that arise. We encourage each other to strive for greatness. We bring everything we can to the relationship, knowing that our spouse is doing the same. It's a commitment we've made to each other.

THE LESSON

We all deserve happiness, and it is out there. The sad truth is we don't find love as easily as movies would have us believe. For most, there will be failed attempts, but I promise you that happiness is out there for everyone. Finding the right spouse does not mean there won't be arguments. In a good relationship, it means the arguments will not tear apart your foundation. We should accept nothing less than someone who loves us and treats us as the Lord would have us to be treated.

To honestly know what it means to have a strong foundation in a relationship, we don't have to look any further than our Heavenly Father. He gives us the perfect example of what we should look for and what we should expect.

- He loves us
- He's faithful to us
- He protects us
- He sacrificed for us
- He's there for us because He wants to be, not because He has to be

All He wants in return is for us to love Him. When we are baptized, we commit to Him. Sometimes, in this commitment, just like in marriage, we get caught up in all the good things and forget there will also be some struggles. God doesn't promise smooth sailing for Christians, but He does promise a solid, unwavering foundation.

A CALL TO ACTION

I'm going to level with you on this one. I'm no relationship counselor. I can say that every day I give my marriage my best effort because of the love I have for my husband. This call to action is for you to be a rock for others. Be someone who finds their strength in God so that others can lean on you in time of need. The second part of this call to action is to identify who the rocks are in your life.

SCRIPTURES

- ❖ Genesis 2:24
- ❖ Ecclesiastes 4:9
- ❖ Mark 10:9
- ❖ Psalm 18:2
- ❖ Psalm 62:1-2
- ❖ Luke 6:47-48

PRAYER

Lord, thank You for showing me how I am to love. Thank You for showing me the love I should expect to receive.

Acknowledgments

To my husband, John Davis

Honey, I don't know how to thank you. You are no-nonsense when I need you to be and playful when I need you to be. Just like my mom used to say about my dad, watching you walk in the door coming home from work at the end of the day feels like Christmas. I don't know how you did it. I don't know how you could see past everything I felt was wrong with myself and pick out what was right. You were exactly who I needed in my life to push me to be more than I had settled on becoming. Thank you for encouraging me in everything I do. You give me the courage to take chances to just *"Silvia that mess"* and not stress over success or failure. I am eternally grateful to you and for you. I love you.

To my Mama, Annie Crawford

Mama, I miss you every single day. I count myself as blessed because you were my mother. I miss calling you on Thanksgiving Day, and I sorely miss laughing with you. I've never known anyone who could laugh at themselves the way you could. You had the rare ability to allow us to laugh at the silly things you would do without taking it personally, and those moments have led to some of our family's most cherished memories. You loved us fiercely, and all six of us know how much better our lives are because of you. We miss you and love you.

To my Daddy, Eldolgie Crawford

Daddy, thank you for being that example. Thank you for making sure five children were up and dressed for church every Sunday morning and Wednesday evening. There is no better gift you can give someone than helping them to understand the need for God to be in their life. You started me on that path. I joke about your lectures, but in honesty, I'm thankful for them. I'm grateful for your willingness to always be open and honest with us, even when we didn't want to hear it. I am especially thankful for how you loved Mom and took care of her. I know she was your world, and I also know you were hers. I love you.

To my first sister and very first roommate, Leslie Wyatt

Les, girl! I love you so much. I'll admit, growing up, I wished you away a couple of times because I wanted my own room, but I'm glad those wishes never came true. How we both can take a stand when irritated and how we can be so opposite from each other and still get along is a true testimony to what it means to be sisters. A few times in this book, I've said that you should have been the big sister, and maybe I'm not the only one who felt that way. It would explain why everybody in the house, when attempting to say my name, would start by saying yours and why I had to learn to start answering to the name, Les-Silvia. Ugh!!!!! Despite it all, I'm glad you are my big little sister.

To my second sister, Lucretia Yates

Cre, girl! I love you so much. You were every bit of what they say a middle child is. The teasing, and fights, and drama that added to the household because of you were crazy! I have no idea how you turned out to be the awesome person you are today. You've always wanted proof of the abuse in writing, so here it is. I'm sorry I held you down while Gina mopped your face with a dirty mop from dirty water. Do with this admission what you will.

To my third sister, Eldolgina Crawford

Gina, girl! I love you so much. You made Mom and Dad work, for sure, but you've become an amazing woman! The confidence you grasp to do the things you want to do is astounding. From the moment I told you I wanted to write this book, you were there encouraging me and never missed an opportunity to tell me how proud you were. Not only did you inspire me with your words, but you did so with your actions. I've watched as you have worked tirelessly over the last few years to get your own business off the ground, and you've done it almost single-handedly. It's beyond Empressive!

To my brother, Wesley Crawford

Bruh! Ditto. Because I left home when you were just starting to come into your own, it took a minute for me to see you as more than just my goofy little brother. Right before I left home, you were the one doing his best to embarrass me by dancing like Michael Jackson in the middle of Mervyn's, but when I came back to visit, instead of seeing my little brother, there was this dude! I'm super proud of the man you became. You were on your own earlier than any of the rest of us, and you stayed that way. I know that wasn't easy, but you did it! I don't think I would have done as good of a job at that as you did. I admire you more than you know.

To my son, Jacob Larsen

The day you were born was the scariest day of my life. I couldn't believe there were no tests I had to pass to prove I could take care of something so precious. You brought joy into my life, the likes of which I had never known, and 25 years later, you still do. Thank you for trusting me and sometimes following my advice based solely on that trust. Thank you for finding such a wonderful woman with whom to share your life. Alma makes it so very easy for me to love her. You have no idea how often we hear from those who have met you what an awesome young man you are. Your smile, your laugh, how you interact with people, these are indeed your gifts. Thank you for making being a parent so easy and for the new kind of love you brought into my life. Thanks for making me a mom, the best thing I could ever have hoped to be. I love you. And no pressure, but feel free to make me a grandmother as soon as you like.

To my daughter, Jordan Larsen

Baby girl, the day you were born, I expected I'd be better prepared. I'd been through having a child once and thought how different could the experience be? As it turns out, very! This time I had a little girl, and you were different from your brother in multiple ways. Where Jacob had gotten us used to a child who screamed in his crib until he fell asleep, you quietly would roll over and drift off, and that was just the beginning of a world of differences. You've wanted to be an adult for as long as I can remember. You wanted to be grown so badly you didn't even wait the whole nine months to be born and came into this world as a preemie. Guiding you during your teenage years felt like we were forcing a race car built for speed to pace itself at 25 mph. Watching you deal with the pain you experience while you push through to get the things you want out of life has put me in awe of you in ways I can't explain. You test me, and you strengthen me. You encourage me. You're my friend, and I love you. (not to ever be confused with one of yo little friends, though).

To Josh Gordon

I'm so glad I asked if you would be willing to give your advice. Your knowledge of the Word and scripture references were a tremendous help. Thank you for your thoughtful insights, for challenging my views, and for helping me better shape and convey my ideas. And thank you for being a boss at grammar!

To my Aunt Patricia Walker and to Ray and Verda Johnson

You each took time out of your schedules and read every single chapter as they were developed, and provided your feedback for me to ponder. I needed that encouragement because this was a scary undertaking at times. Thank you so much.

To Nicole

Well, you know. :)

To The Father, The Son, and The Holy Spirit

I love You.